Keeping Employees Accountable for Results

Quick Tips for Busy Managers

Brian Cole Miller

AMACOM

American Management Association

New York · Atlanta · Brussels · Chicago · Mexico City · San Francisco
Shanghai · Tokyo · Toronto · Washington, D.C.

Special discounts on bulk quantities of AMACOM books are available to corporations, professional associations, and other organizations. For details, contact Special Sales Department, AMACOM, a division of American Management Association, 1601 Broadway, New York, NY 10019.
Tel.: 212-903-8316. Fax: 212-903-8083.
Web site: www.amacombooks.org

This publication is designed to provide accurate and authoritative information in regard to the subject matter covered. It is sold with the understanding that the publisher is not engaged in rendering legal, accounting, or other professional service. If legal advice or other expert assistance is required, the services of a competent professional person should be sought.

Library of Congress Cataloging-in-Publication Data

Miller, Brian Cole, 1956–
    Keeping employees accountable for results : quick tips for busy managers /
Brian Cole Miller.
      p.   cm.
   Includes index.
   ISBN 0-8144-7320-2
   1. Performance standards.   2. Goal setting in personnel
management.   I. Title.
   HF5549.5.P35M55   2006
   658.3' 125—dc22

2005024601

Printing number

10 9 8 7 6 5 4 3 2 1

Keeping Employees Accountable for Results

CONTENTS

ACKNOWLEDGMENTS

Thank you to the busy managers and professionals who took time to read my manuscript and give me such valuable insight and feedback, including Rachel Cope, Lynn Jackson, Chris Kennedy, Dean Miller, Alex Rodriguez, Wendy Shaw, and Dawn Snyder. Also, thank you, Adrienne Hickey, for your patience and understanding through the rough times.

Thank you, Lisa Alexander, for demonstrating to me how to receive feedback. I've never met anyone so addicted to it!

Thank you, Wendy Shaw, for showing me that measurement maniacs can be such fun people!

Thank you, Patty Skerritt, for showing me how this stuff works in the real world. You are one great manager!

Thank you, Garbage. I listened to you constantly while I wrote. I bet you never imagined your music could inspire someone while writing a business book!

Thank you, Chris Kennedy, for teaching me several important lessons about accountability. And thanks for believing in me, my friend!

Thank you, Lynn Jackson, for caring enough and having the courage to give me that extremely difficult feedback about the flow of my third (and what I thought was last) draft. I love you, Sis!

A special thank you goes to my family—Logan, Heidee, Benjamin, Gail, Wayne, and Dean. Your support, encouragement, and confidence simply overwhelm me!

And most of all, thank you, Tim.

Keeping Employees Accountable for Results

This book is written for the busy manager who wants to maximize employee and team productivity through accountability.

The principles in the book are not exclusively for the busy manager, however. Anyone can use them with a boss, peers, vendors, consultants, and business partners. You can even apply them outside the job. Use them to hold contractors, lawyers, designers, community leaders, mechanics, your teenagers, and just about anyone else in your life accountable.

While this book includes a process, several pieces can be used separately. For example, providing feedback is useful in many other day-to-day activities. Praise your son's success in school, recognize your niece's efforts in her lacrosse game, or complain to a restaurant manager about poor service.

What You Can Expect from This Book

Heavy on application, light on theory, this book focuses on how-tos. It includes steps, tips, and examples throughout. You'll learn what to do, when to do it, and how to do it. What you won't find is a lot of theory. I've included just enough to validate the how-tos but not enough to make you an expert on the subject. Busy managers don't have time for that. "Just give me what I need to get the job done!" is what I hear most from my clients, whether large or small, for-profit or not-for-profit.

In each chapter here's what you'll see (and not see):

- *Lots of examples.* Wherever possible I've shown one or more examples of the particular step or point. Most of them are from real companies or real-life experiences.
- *Some theory, but not a lot.* I've included just enough to help the steps make sense, and to justify their order.
- *Not every possibility is covered.* If it were, this book would be several volumes long. I've covered the most common circum-

stances. If yours are different, either ask someone for help (you can call me at Working Solutions) or get one of those long, drawn-out books.

- *An easy-to-read format.* It highlights the basics so that you can easily skim past stuff you already know.
- *Details when you need them.* You can delve deeper when you want more specifics and go right back to a higher level when you've had enough.
- *A conversational style.* It's simple and makes for a quick read.

The SIMPLE Approach to Accountability

Accountability is a process that consists of six principles. Each principle builds on the previous one.

S = Set Expectations. Your employees need to know what is expected of them before you can hold them accountable for anything. You can't assume they know what is supposed to be done, when, or to what quality level. The more clearly you set expectations and goals up front, the less time you will waste later clarifying—or worse, arguing—about what was really expected.

I = Invite Commitment. Just because your employees know what to do doesn't mean they will do it. After they understand what the goals and expectations are, they need to commit to achieving them. They are more likely to do this when they buy in to two things: how the goals will benefit them personally, and how the goals will help move the organization forward. When this connection is made, they will commit to the goals. They will welcome your holding them accountable for their results.

M = Measure Results. You need information to hold your employees accountable. You will measure their performance so that you can gauge whether they've met the goals and expectations that they committed to. Goals aren't measurable unless they are quantifiable, and all goals can be made quantifiable. Measure the results and compare them to your employees' goals to find the gaps that require further attention.

P = Provide Feedback. Share the information you've gathered with your employees. Feedback doesn't solve problems by itself. It opens the door for problem-solving discussions and follow-up actions. Your employees cannot do a good job without feedback, and they certainly can't improve without it. Most of the time, giving feedback is all it takes. Setting expectations followed by quality feedback is the backbone of holding someone accountable for results.

L = Link to Consequences. Sometimes your employees will need a little more help to live up to their commitments. When they struggle to reach their goals, you can help them by administering appropriate consequences. Don't confuse consequences with punishments, though. Punishments are inflicted on employees to make them pay for their shortcomings. They do not contribute to a solution. Consequences, however, will guide and focus employees' behavior and encourage them to take their commitments more seriously.

E = Evaluate Effectiveness. After you have worked with the principles of accountability for a while, you need to evaluate how your efforts have paid off. Determine if you were successful at holding your employees accountable to reach the goals that were set. And in the spirit of continuous improvement, review how you handled the process. Find ways to be more effective at applying the principles of accountability. Hold yourself accountable for holding others accountable!

Each chapter covers one principle of SIMPLE. Each principle is divided into several how-to steps. Each step is presented in the same easy-to-read (and even easier-to-skim) format:

THE STEP describes what the step is in one sentence.

THE REASONS section explains why the step is important.

THE BASICS section covers the highlights of how to do the step or the essentials to keep in mind while doing it.

THE DETAILS section delivers all the background information about the step, substeps, examples, variations of the step, and things to be cautious about.

At the end of each chapter is a CHECKLIST that will give you the highlights of what is covered in that chapter. Use this to make sure you understand all the main points before moving on.

How to Use This Book

◆ **This book is organized so that you can readily get as much or as little information as you want.** You can skim at a high level without missing the essentials. Just read the Steps, Reasons, and Basics in each chapter. When something grabs your attention, it is easy to dive deep into the Details right there.

◆ **Examples are spread throughout the book.** They are displayed in a way that makes it easy to pick them out quickly. Generally, they illustrate the point being made in the text preceding them.

There is a long example at the end of Chapter 2. It shows the conclusion of all the work done in chapters 1 and 2. The other long example is at the end of Chapter 5. This one demonstrates how several steps in chapters 4 and 5 might be used together in a real-life situation.

◆ **This book is written as a process, but several pieces of that process can stand alone.** For example, you can apply the principles of SMART goals to business planning, project management, employee development planning, personal goal setting, succession planning, and more.

◆ **This book will not help you much with your superstars.** If you want to manage your superstars better, get a book about rewards and recognition. That said, is this book all about problem employees? Not really. Sure, you will learn how to deal with those problem employees. But more important, this book is about helping you set your employees up for success so that none of them ever becomes a problem employee!

◆ **This book outlines an ideal process that may not always jibe with the real world you live in.** I recognize this and realize that you may not be able to follow every step presented here. I considered trying to anticipate every possible contingency and addressing it. Rather, I chose to trust that you wouldn't have the title "manager" if you didn't already know how to adapt or go with something that was less than a perfect fit.

Use the steps as a model or a pattern to follow when they make sense for you. Adjust your approach when they don't pertain. I have confidence that you, Busy Manager, can take what is relevant and use that to become an even better manager.

CHAPTER 1

Set Expectations

The success of any organization comes down to one thing: how well it organizes its members to focus on and work toward the same purpose. Assuming an organization knows what that thing is, and communicates it well, your staff members should be focused on doing their part in that effort. If your staff members don't contribute to that aim, they're probably not doing the right work!

Step 1. Determine what your organization wants to accomplish.

The Reasons

Everything done anywhere in the organization should link back to what it has declared is its most important work. So start at the top. Organizations use different methods to identify what's most important—missions, visions, strategies, objectives, goals, and values are the most common. Each has a slightly different meaning and a slightly different emphasis that will help you get clear about the focus of your organization. Your organization's focus doesn't merely set the context for holding your employees accountable; it should drive it!

The Basics

1. Review all of your organization's mission statements, vision statements, values, strategies, goals, and objectives.

2. Get a full and complete picture of where your organization is, why it is, and where it's going, as well as how it intends to get there.

The Details

A **mission statement** is a brief statement of the organization's reason for being. It is used to help keep an organization focused on what is (and what is not) its work. Here are some examples:

- To extend and enhance human life by providing the highest-quality pharmaceutical and related health care products. (*Bristol-Myers Squibb Company, a pharmaceutical company*)
- To help leaders become more confident and competent at the front line. (*Working Solutions, a leadership consulting firm*)
- To improve the quality of life for our customers, team members, suppliers, shareholders, and communities where we have facilities through the effective operation of profitable, diversified, yet balanced businesses that extend worldwide. (*Koch Enterprises, a diversified holding company*)

Don't confuse a mission statement with an organization's tagline. The mission statement tells why the organization exists. The tagline will create interest in the organization.

- The mission of TeamBaldwin CPAs is: *To provide our clients with financial peace of mind while providing an enjoyable work environment for our team members.*
- The tagline for TeamBaldwin CPAs is: *Making Business and Taxes Fun.*

If your organization has no mission statement, you can approximate one quickly. Ask yourself, "Why do we exist as an organization? What is our purpose for being?" Don't get confused by things like making a profit, dominating market share, or beating out the competition. Although important, these are rarely the true reasons an organization exists. They are more likely goals or strategies than mission statements. For the organization's mission statement, seek to understand the core reason for its existence. You don't need verbiage. Quite the contrary, you should be able to summarize your organization's mission in fewer than 50 words.

In larger organizations, smaller parts of that organization may have their own mission statements that reflect what their contribution to the overall organization is. For example, the cafeteria at an automotive parts factory might have a mission statement something like:

> To provide nutritious, affordable meals to factory workers in a clean and pleasant environment.

If your department or unit doesn't have a mission statement, you can create one by asking similar questions to the ones on page 8. "Why do we exist as a work group? What is our department's purpose for being? What do we contribute to our organization?" For instance:

> Why do we exist as an organization?
> *As the Labor Relations Group, we help our internal clients steer clear of labor litigation.*

> What is our purpose?
> *To investigate discrimination complaints. To educate our management team about how to follow employment laws.*

> What else?
> *To make sure sexual harassment doesn't happen in the workplace.*

Given all this, the mission statement might be:

> To help make our organization one that welcomes and values all workers of all kinds.

Vision, in contrast to mission, is a verbal picture of a desired future state for the organization. A vision statement is used to in-

spire employees to strive for an ideal. For example, the vision for
Lincoln Electric, a manufacturer of welding equipment, is:

> Lincoln Electric will be the undisputed world leader in the arc
> welding industry as measured by global sales volume, while si-
> multaneously aiming to maximize shareholder value.
>
> We will be the leader in supplying the finest-quality welding
> and cutting products. In order to accomplish this, we will con-
> tinue our emphasis on being the industry's lowest-cost pro-
> ducer, on providing applications expertise and solutions for our
> customers, and on developing new and innovative technology
> that responds to customer needs with value-added products
> and services.

If your organization (or department or unit) has no vision, ask
yourself these questions: "What do we want this organization to
look like in *x* years? In what ways do we want to be better than we
are now? What do we want to have accomplished by then?"

> What do we want this organization to look like five years from
> now?
> ▪ *An environment free of threats and intimidation*
> ▪ *No sexual-harassment complaints or lawsuits*
> ▪ *A place where men and women of any sexual orientation can
>   work together without concern for personal safety or comfort*

Longer than a mission statement, the vision is something of a
narrative or series of bullet points. Vivid and alive, it should describe what the organization will be like in the future from a positive, affirming perspective. Given this, the vision for the Labor
Relations Group might include statements like the following:

> *We support a harassment-free environment as evidenced by the
> lack of formal and informal complaints or lawsuits. We are seen
> as a model for integrating women into nontraditional jobs in our
> industry.*

Values are principles or standards for conduct common across the organization. Whereas mission and vision statements describe where the company is and where it's going, values describe how the company achieves these goals. The statement of values anchors employees' behavior during the course of normal business, as well as in times of stress, change, or turmoil. Here is a list of values for Nationwide Insurance:

Performance Values
We have a bias for action and a passion for results.
We act accountably.
We value coaching and feedback.
We work as one team.
We have fun.

Core Values
We value people.
We are customer-focused.
We act with honesty and integrity.
We trust and respect each other.

If your organization has no stated values, ask yourself, "How do we believe we should work with each other? What ethics or ideals do we share? How do we believe our work should be conducted?" Values can be statements like the example above or simply a list of attributes.

Values for the College of Dentistry, University of Florida
- Excellence
- Integrity
- Fairness
- Communication
- Cooperation
- Courtesy
- Continuous improvement

Strategies, goals, and objectives are an organization's statements of its intent or focus. These statements describe tangible results the organization aspires to. The highest level or most broadly stated focus is called a strategy. Strategies usually deal with things like market share, revenues, operating costs, sales, service levels, grant levels, membership numbers, and so on. The strategy is used to drive goals and tactics further down in the organization. Here's an abbreviated list of strategies for Compuware, a software company:

- We will provide service to all customers beyond their expectations.
- We will increasingly focus on new markets and customers while maintaining strong relationships with existing customers.
- We will view our diversity as a corporate asset, utilizing the strength it creates in our business and community.
- We will respect our employees and provide them with opportunities to grow and share in the success of Compuware.
- We will regard our vendors as strategic partners and remain committed to strengthening these relationships through mutual respect, trust, and goal satisfaction.
- We will be sensitive to costs, knowing that an efficient organization will benefit our customers, our corporation, and its employees.
- We will continue to pursue all opportunities for growth that are consistent with our long-term financial health.

Terms like *goal, objective, deliverable,* and *target* then are used to break down a strategy into more tangible, bite-size results.

For example, Compuware's strategy to provide its employees with opportunities to share in the success of Compuware may be broken down into a few goals or targets. These may be to institute programs for profit sharing, annual bonuses, or individual recognition. Any of those programs could be further broken down into specific deliverables of what the program may look like, when it will be ready, how much it will cost, and so on.

If your organization has no stated strategies, goals, or objectives, ask yourself, "What specifically do we want to accomplish in the short and long term? What should we achieve? What major steps must we take to be successful?" Start with high-level strategy statements. Then break those down into smaller, more manageable statements of intent.

Step 2. Determine what part of your organization's success is your team's responsibility.

The Reasons

Unless you are a very small enterprise, the work of an organization must be divided up among groups to get it all done. Divvying up the work like this allows each group to focus on its part and be successful. Only when each manager accepts responsibility for getting his or her piece of that work done can the organization prosper as a whole.

The Basics

1. If you have already been handed a pile of work to be responsible for, you are done with this step.
2. If not, you will have to define (or negotiate) your group's workload yourself. Based on your organization's direction (see step 1), ask yourself and other stakeholders, "What part of the whole do we affect? Which resources do we control that can affect the bottom line? What will others expect of us? What should we do to move things along? How are others dependent on us?"
3. The final question to ask yourself before moving on is this: "Given all this, how realistic are the expectations of our work group?" Make sure you believe they can be accomplished. If you don't, your employees won't. If they don't, it won't happen.

The Details

Don't become overwhelmed or overloaded. There always seems to be more work than is possible to get done. Prioritizing and saying no are difficult for most managers. Prioritize now, say no now, and push back now. You're going to have to push back sometime. Why not do it now with forethought and planning, rather than in the heat of the moment, shooting from the hip? Then, from a position of rational thinking, stand up for yourself and your staff so you don't burn anyone out down the road.

The reality is that you may not get anywhere by pushing back. At least you raised the flag early, and others have been put on notice that everything may not be possible by the deadlines given to you.

Check your resources. Time, technology, money, data, supplies, and equipment are only some of the resources you will want to be sure are in place or available for your group to perform its work. Your group cannot be expected to do the work required without proper resources, so make sure they are properly lined up. If they are not, now is the time to get them or to push back on the organization's expectations of your group.

Step 3. Determine what part of your team's results you will hold each individual accountable for.

The Reasons

Teamwork is great, but when it comes to holding people accountable, you have to go to individuals—even when you are holding them accountable for being good team players. Expectations of each team member may or may not be the same. And regardless, their contributions are never identical, so you should not treat them as such.

Each individual must be held accountable for his own performance. This can't happen if the group's work has not been divvied up for individual team-member accountability. Each employee must know what part of the team's results is his to accomplish personally.

The Basics

1. Sometimes it's as easy as taking the team's goals and dividing them equally among the team members:

   - The team goal is to handle 45 calls per hour. Each of the five phone reps is then expected to average nine calls per hour.
   - The team goal is to seat each guest as she arrives. Each of the 14 ushers takes turns seating guests and returning to the line until all guests have been seated.
   - The team goal is to sell 16 manicures to current clients this week. Each of the four stylists is then expected to sell four manicures.

2. Usually it is not that simple or straightforward, though. If not, you, the manager, are required to make the call. Just make sure that when the work is divided up, nothing is left unassigned.
3. Assigning responsibilities is ultimately your job, but that doesn't mean you have to do it alone. This may be a perfect time for you to get input from your team on how to divide up the work.

The Details

Consider the following as you parcel out the team's responsibilities to individual team members.

- *Union contracts.* Your decision might be made for you by union contracts or other agreements that already spell out what should be required of whom. Always check carefully before making any changes.
- *Experience.* How long someone has been doing a particular job or function may dictate what can or should be required

of her. With experience usually comes speed, accuracy, quality, and a capacity for greater performance. Don't be afraid to challenge an individual by raising the bar.

- *Expertise.* This is different from merely having done something (experience); it is about how well the individual can perform a task regardless of experience level. Leverage each person's skill level for maximum group performance.

- *Overlap.* It is difficult to hold employees accountable when responsibility is spread out, loosely shared, or otherwise unclear. Finger pointing becomes too easy. As much as possible, make sure work responsibilities are clearly divided or defined.

- *Resources.* The available technology, supplies, equipment, data, timelines, and so on (or lack thereof) may play into what you can expect from various individuals in your group.

- *Position/level/salary.* Designations such as "senior" or "lead" should be respected and leveraged appropriately. Those who earn a higher salary also deserve to have higher expectations placed on them.

- *History.* Precedents may be set on who does what. Don't feel bound by the past, but respect it and take what's worked before into consideration.

Step 4. Determine who should write your employees' goals.

The Reasons

Deciding what work belongs to whom is one thing. Articulating the work to be done in a clear and concise way is another task altogether. There are pros and cons as to whether you or your employees should write the goals. You'll want to be deliberate in deciding who will do this task so you maximize the benefits from it.

The Basics

1. Consider the pros and cons of who writes the goals, and select which are more important here.

2. A collaborative approach is usually best. Balance your and your employees' input into this process so that you can leverage the benefits available from each.

The Details

Traditionally, managers write their employees' goals. However, there are several good reasons to consider having your employees write their own goals.

- *They will buy into them more strongly.* Your employees are more likely to accept and commit to reaching goals that they write themselves. Increase your employees' commitment by involving them in the goal-setting process as much as possible.
- *The burden is off of you.* The bulk of the work is on their shoulders. Yes, you have to review the goals they write. You may have to change or negotiate a few goals. But for the most part, the workload falls to your employees.
- *They learn new skills.* Your employees develop skills while writing their goals—planning, organization, analysis, work breakdown structures, measurement, reporting, and documentation, to name just a few. After they write a draft and get input from you, they will learn about adjusting their thinking, being flexible, and negotiating outcomes, too.
- *They better appreciate your role in holding them accountable for results.* When they are forced to consider for themselves what needs to be done, when, and how, there will be fewer surprises down the road. They can see how you will monitor their performance and what specifically you will be looking for.
- *They better understand their roles by putting them into words.* Their struggle to identify how to make their goals measurable helps them see even better what they need to accomplish. The process clarifies for them exactly how you will determine if they indeed do accomplish their goals.

- *They are more realistic.* They probably know the job better than you. Based on personal experience, they are in a better position to be more realistic than you might be. They can put all the pieces into context and see conflicts and overlaps that you might not see.
- *They feel encouraged by your show of confidence.* You are never accused of being autocratic or dictatorial when your employees help write their own goals. Asking for their input demonstrates your confidence in their understanding of their own jobs and how they fit within the organization.

Of course, writing employees' goals yourself has its benefits too.

- *You maintain complete control.* By writing the goals yourself, you can craft them exactly as you want them. You can make sure they focus on what you want, what you need. You can make them as difficult or easy as you like.
- *It's faster to do them yourself than to collaborate.* You know what you are doing and how to do it. You don't have to spend time coaching your employee on how to do it, or negotiating items that he includes or excludes. You can work on your schedule and at your own pace.
- *It's just easier to do it alone.* The more input you get, the more complex the final result will be in order to accommodate different perspectives. Doing it alone saves having to integrate input and suggestions.
- *You will get to know their jobs better.* As you study what needs to be done, how, and when, you can't help but learn the job more intimately. You'll be in a better position down the road to hold your employees accountable for results.

Be aware that the cost of these benefits is high. You risk losing all the benefits of collaboration and perhaps even alienating your employees or creating unnecessary resentment. No matter who your employee is, you should be able to find a way to include him when writing his goals.

Step 5. Use SMART to define each employee's responsibilities with goals that are SPECIFIC.

In developing effective goals, use the acronym SMART. Goals must be Specific, Measurable, Action-oriented, Realistic, and Time-bound. You can't hold people accountable for not meeting expectations they weren't aware of. SMART represents an effective tool for describing exactly what you expect from each individual.

The Reasons

Specific. The more specific a goal, the more likely the success. Specificity takes the guesswork out. You don't find yourself saying to your employees, "Well, *this* is not what I meant!" Nor will you often hear, "Well, why didn't you say you wanted *that?*"

You set everyone up for true accountability by being specific from the very beginning.

The Basics

1. Start with a goal, stated as broadly as you like.
2. Ask, "What do I mean by that? What would success in this goal look like if I saw it happening? What would I observe? What would I hear?"
3. Keep asking those questions to further specify your goal.
4. When you are able to pinpoint the behaviors that require no further questions to spell out what is expected of your employee, you're specific enough. Here's an example:

Start with the goal broadly stated: "Demonstrate initiative regularly."

What would success look like?
My employees would use the Suggestion Program.

What do I mean by "using" the Suggestion Program?
Employees would submit good ideas, ones they care about.

What do I mean by that?
They would care enough to be willing to take the lead on trying out the suggestions they submit.

So a more specific goal could be: "Demonstrate initiative not only by suggesting ways to improve the work (via the Suggestion Program), but also by taking the lead on implementing those suggestions, at least to start out."

The Details

Often, more than one answer comes from the above questions. A simple, broad, or vague goal may turn into many smaller goals. These multiple goals, specific as they are, are much more likely to be met than the broad, vague goal that spawned them. Now is not the time to strive for brevity. But it's not all about quantity, either. Even more important is the quality—meaning specificity—as in this example:

Start with "Develop yourself by constantly upgrading your skills."

What do I mean by that?
My employees take advantage of all the training our organization offers.

What would success look like?
My employees attend training and encourage others to do so.

What else would success look like?
My employees also apply what they learn in the training to their day-to-day jobs.

What else would I observe?
My employees can and do identify their own developmental needs.

So, "Develop yourself by constantly upgrading your skills" could change into "Take advantage of at least 75 percent of applicable training offered here; apply what is learned in training on the job; create a personal development plan each quarter." One vague goal became three more specific ones.

For the most part, goals are specific when they abandon value statements or generalizations for concrete behavioral statements:

Rather than "Show good teamwork" (general), a specific goal would be "Help with your teammates' backlog when your workload permits."

Even more specific would be "Help your teammates by processing at least ten of the oldest invoices in queue when you finish sorting the mail and before you do the department filing."

Specific goals take the wiggle room out of accountability. Unfortunately, most managers tend to make vague or general requests of their staff and assume staff members know how to translate those statements into behaviors, as in this example:

"Be customer focused."

Does "Be customer focused" mean giving customers what they say they want (just take the order)? Or does it mean consulting with customers to help them get what they truly need? Or does it mean something in between? Different industries may answer this clarifying question differently—and appropriately so.

When confronted for lacking customer focus, an employee could rightfully argue, "What do you mean? I am always friendly, smiling, and pleasant to the customers! I give them exactly what they ask for. If that's not customer focus, I don't know what is!" You know you've not been specific enough when that's not at all what you meant by "Be customer focused." You (and your employee) get a better feel for what you meant when you respond, "Well, that's nice, yes. But what we really need for you to do is help the customer by offering menu items that would complement their selections appropriately. Sometimes they don't realize how well a particular side dish would set off a steak, for example. So from now on, when a customer orders . . ."

The conversation would be very different if the goal had originally been stated as, "After receiving the customer's order, offer at least one menu item that would complement that order." The employee either did or did not offer the complementary menu item. In that case, you would both discuss that behavior factually, and not argue about the interpretation of what is or is not meant by "customer focus."

Be specific now, not later. Rather than have that discussion of clarification later (and as part of an unnecessary confrontation), have it now, alone, before it even becomes an issue with you and your employees. Get crystal clear yourself. It will be easy to then be clear with your employees and set them up for success. They will know exactly what is expected of them, and there will be no room for interpretation, guesswork, or trial and error.

This takes more time and effort, but it pays off in the end. You won't argue about what you meant by goals (usually finding yourself on the defensive side of that argument), and you won't lose time starting over with revised goals. You won't even give that occasional game-player of an employee a playing field. It will be clear from the start.

Step 6. Use SMART to define each employee's responsibilities with goals that are MEASURABLE.

The Reasons

Measurable. This goes hand in hand with specificity. While specific goals help clarify the "what" of a goal, measurable goals clarify the "how much," "how well," or "to what level or degree" of a goal. Measuring takes the guesswork out of determining if a goal was actually achieved or not. It helps you assess both quantity and quality. You don't find yourself saying, "Well, this isn't the quality I was looking for." Nor will you often hear, "I had no idea you wanted it done like *that!*"

The Basics

1. Start with a goal, stated as broadly as you like.
2. Ask, "How will I know when this has been accomplished well? What would real success look like? What will I see and hear—or not—that indicates success (or failure)? What's an objective way we can use to evaluate this? How would I know if this was not done well?"
3. Keep asking those questions.
4. When you get to answers that you can count, the goal is measurable. For example:

Start with the goal broadly stated: "Manage the schedule for conference rooms A and B."

What would success look like?
Two meetings are never scheduled in the same room at the same time.

How would I know if this is not done well?
I receive complaints about scheduling problems.

How else will I know when this is done well?
No one complains to me.

How else will I know when this is done well?
My employee spends little time fixing mix-ups or other problems.

The original goal could be restated as "Manage conference rooms A and B so that three or fewer scheduling complaints come to my attention this year." While it certainly does not measure everything, it gets at the most obvious measure.

The Details

To be measurable, a goal must be quantifiable. This is easy for obviously countable behaviors like sales, number of widgets, or speed.

- Land six new accounts this year.
- Input 23 orders per minute.
- Greet customers within three minutes of their being seated at your table.

It becomes more difficult with behaviors that are tougher to count, but it is still possible. For example:

"Make presentations that are well organized" is not easily measurable. A measurable goal would be "In your presentations, use no more than three index cards of notes, maintain eye contact with the audience 90 percent of the time, and say 'um' or 'uh' fewer than five times." Things that indicate an organized presentation are now quantified.

Measures take the wiggle room out of accountability. Unfortunately, most managers tend to make vague quality demands of their staff and then assume staff members know how to translate those statements into the level of quality the manager wants or needs.

"Run the weekly cross-team update meeting effectively."
How do you measure "effectively?" Does it mean starting and ending on time? Or does it mean an agenda is distributed beforehand and then strictly followed? Or does it mean making sure everyone enjoys the meeting? Or does it mean something else altogether?

When confronted for running ineffective meetings, an employee might retort, "What do you mean? We never went late. We always followed the agenda. Everyone got to speak who wanted to. We distributed the minutes within days of each meeting. How can you say my meetings weren't effective?" You haven't applied appropriate measures; the employee didn't understand what you meant by "effectively." Both of you get a better feel for a true measure for this goal when you respond, "Well, those are all important elements of running a meeting, yes. What really matters most, though, is the outcome of the meeting. Here, we want all team representatives who attend to leave with the information about the project that they need to keep their own departments informed and . . ."

The conversation would be very different if the original goal had been stated as "Run the weekly cross-team update meeting so that all attendees leave with the info they need to take meaningful action to keep the project at or under budget." The attendees either did or did not have the information they needed to proceed with the project. You know whether they did or not by the biweekly budget reports, the lack of follow-up questions from them later on, or by asking them directly if they are getting what they need from the meetings. You should be talking about those measurable results— quantifiably—and not arguing about what makes a meeting more "effective" than something else.

Discuss clarification now, not later, before it becomes a bone of contention. Get clear on it together. What do you mean by those vague labels thrown all over their job duties? You both need to know precisely what level of performance is expected. Leave no room for misunderstandings or guesswork.

The ideal measure would be all of the following:

* Inexpensive
* Automatic
* Unbiased
* Quick and immediate
* Require minimal effort
* Simple/uncomplicated
* Few exceptions to the rule
* A true measure of what's being evaluated

Rarely will you find a measure that has all those attributes. Look for measures that have as many as possible and your success at holding people accountable for results will be greatly improved. Don't fear having to argue about what quality or quantity you meant by the goals, nor about whether conclusions you've drawn from their performance are fair and accurate. Your level of expectations, as well as how you'd determine their success, will be clear from the start.

You set everyone up for true accountability when your goals have clear measures from the beginning.

Step 7. Use SMART to define each employee's responsibilities with goals that are ACTION-ORIENTED.

The Reasons

Action-Oriented. Goals that are action-oriented help keep the focus where it should be: on the employee's behavior. Actions and behaviors are measurable. Things like attitudes, efforts, and intentions are not. You don't struggle to interpret why the employee did this or that. You don't find yourself saying, "Hmm, I wonder if this means she's not very committed to the project?" Nor will you hear, "Just because I was late doesn't mean I have a bad attitude!"

The Basics

1. Start with a goal, stated as vaguely as you like.
2. Ask, "What would this look like? How could they prove this to me? How will I know when I see it?"
3. Keep asking those questions.
4. When you get answers that are tangible behaviors or results, your goals are action-oriented. For example:

Start with a goal, however vague: "Be helpful with new members of the team."

What would "helpful" look like?
My employee would introduce the new employee to key contacts.

What else would this look like?
My employee would take the new employee on a plant tour.

How could this prove to be helpful?
The new employee does not come to me with minor questions and issues.

How will I know the employee was helpful when I see it?
The new employee adjusts quickly to the new job and knows whom to turn to for various issues.

The original goal could be stated as, "Familiarize new employees with key contacts and locations important to their initial success on the job." Although this doesn't cover every aspect of being helpful, it nails down some specific, measurable behaviors that clarify what is needed.

The Details

Goals are action-oriented when they are grounded in behaviors. This can be a challenging distinction, but it's a critical one. Here's an example:

"Have a compassionate approach toward all patients" is a feeling-based goal. An action-oriented goal would be "Use a calm, reassuring tone of voice with all patients."

Focus action-oriented goals on results, behaviors, or both. Many organizations are heavily results-oriented. Goals are aimed at the end result regardless of how one gets there. The assumption, of course, is that the employee uses legal, ethical, and moral ways to accomplish goals. End-result goals also allow employees greater freedom and creativity in accomplishing their goals, as follows:

"The Product Protection Plan is sold to 14 percent of all electronic equipment customers."
   Your employee may ask every customer to purchase the plan. He or she may ask only those buying big-ticket items. They may ask inoffensively or suggest aggressively. However they do it doesn't matter so long as the sales quota is met.

More and more organizations are caring about not only what is accomplished, but how it is done. Behavioral goals are aimed at how your employees get the result expected of them. Certain behaviors may have been proven to get the results needed. Or they are behaviors that reflect the organization's values or mission:

"Every customer, regardless of purchase, leaves the store with a Product Protection Plan flyer, and every electronics customer is offered the plan with one question, no more."

This pushes behaviors that are believed to produce Product Protection Plan sales. One of the store's values is the "soft sell." Management sets behavioral goals that promote that approach. Of course, this goal may be combined with one requiring a 14 percent sales quota for a new goal that targets both results and behaviors.

Focus goals on what you can observe. You can observe results, actions, and behaviors. When you can observe them, you can count them (measurable). When you can count them, you can hold someone accountable for them. You cannot hold people accountable for something entirely within themselves. Since they alone can understand or confirm what their emotions, feelings, or mental state may be, accountability would be impossible.

Unfortunately, most managers mistakenly believe their job is to hold employees accountable for an emotional or mental state—the most common being attitude. For example:

"Show a good attitude about cleanliness."

What would a good attitude look like? How would you know if employees did have a good attitude? How would you know if they did not? Of course the answers to these questions are the behaviors that are indicative of a good attitude.

Action-oriented goals take the psychological diagnosis out of accountability. When confronted about a bad attitude in the dining room, an employee could rightfully argue, "How on earth do you know if I have a bad attitude? Didn't I clean the tables? Aren't they all spotless? Didn't I do it quickly? If that doesn't show a good attitude, I don't know what does!" You and your employee get a much better feel for what behaviors you expect when you respond, "Well, yes; thank you. The tables are clean and you did do that quickly. What you also did, though, was make disparaging comments about the task to customers eating nearby. You also sighed heavily several times and rolled your eyes to them when they looked up at you. What we really need for you to do is . . ."

The conversation would be very different if the original goal had been stated as "Keep the dining room tables wiped down while pleasantly greeting or smiling at the customers in the room." The employee either did smile or did not. You could be talking about the measurable actions you observed and not arguing about what kind of attitude the employee has. That is an argument you can never win because the employee is the only one who can know the true answer. All you can point at are the behaviors he or she exhibits that suggest what kind of attitude is inside.

Rather than have that argument, be clear now, before it even becomes an issue between you and your employee. What do you mean by a good attitude? Let employees know exactly what behaviors you are expecting. Don't leave the door open to trial and error.

Keep the focus where it belongs: on the employee's actions. Why put yourself in the position of having to make assumptions or inferences, when all you really have to do is define what behaviors you want and let the employee worry about how that translates internally? Spell out the actions you want to see, be specific, and make sure they're measurable, and you're on your way to successful accountability.

Step 8. Use SMART to define each employee's responsibilities with goals that are REALISTIC.

The Reasons

Realistic. When goals are realistic, they keep an employee on track and motivated. When employees hit realistic targets, they gain self-esteem and confidence—confidence in themselves as well as in you. Unreachable goals, however, will not be met. Employees know this and may give up without even trying. If they try and fail, your employees may lose self-esteem and confidence. They may even lose trust in you for expecting the impossible and setting them up for failure.

The Basics

1. Start by stating a goal as high-level as you like.
2. Ask yourself, "How likely is it that this employee can accomplish this? How confident am I that this person can do this? What is the probability of success? Would I be willing to accept less?"
3. Keep asking yourself those questions.
4. When the goal seems reachable by the employee, it is realistic. (Remember, employee capabilities differ, as do confidence levels. What seems realistic for one may appear utterly impossible for another.)
5. Look at all the goals together and make sure they are realistic as a whole. Can one person realistically be expected to accomplish all of them in the time frame given?

The Details

Goals are realistic when both you and your employee truly believe that they can be achieved. There is seldom an absolute borderline between realistic and unrealistic goals. Together you must determine where the line should be drawn.

Realistic goals make it possible to hold employees accountable. The more involved your employee is in writing the goals, the more likely he or she will push to keep them realistic.

Don't be afraid to push a reluctant employee, though. Some employees fear failure so much that they will try to keep the goals as low and unchallenging as possible. Seek a balance between too low a goal and too unrealistically high a goal.

Remember, realistic goals are not universal. What's realistic for one employee may not be realistic for another, as shown below.

"Process 14 claims per hour" may be a realistic stretch goal for an experienced employee. A new employee may find that goal

impossible. "Process six claims per hour" may be a more appropriate, realistic goal for now.

Most managers err by making goals unrealistic, thinking a lofty
goal will inspire an employee to greatness. But see how that back-
fires in this scenario:

An unrealistic goal for a trainer might be "Get an average score
of five out of five on all evaluation sheets for all training delivered
this year." How likely is it that every person in every training
class will give this employee a score of five? How realistic is it
that this employee's performance will be flawless every single
time he delivers training? How likely is it that every attendee will
view the employee's training delivery the same way and rate it
accordingly? What will happen to the employee's motivation
when he gets his first "four" rating from someone? How difficult
would it be to hold someone accountable who has an average
score of 4.99?

When confronted with an average training evaluation score of
4.99, an employee could rightfully argue, "Nobody's perfect, and
to expect such of me was unfair. You can't please all of the people
all of the time. You set me up to fail." Apparently you've not been
realistic in your goals; your employee feels cheated, tricked, or mis-
treated. Your employee will better understand what is realistic when
you relax the standards originally set. "Oh well, no big deal. I figure
that anything above 4.7 is truly outstanding. Actually, anything
above a 4.5 would be a great improvement over last year, and that's
mainly what we were after . . ."

The conversation would have been very different if the original
goal had been "Get an average score of 4.6 out of 5 on all evaluation sheets for all training delivered this year." Or even, "Improve
the average evaluation scores you get this year by 10 percent over
your average last year." The 4.6 (or 10 percent) would be more
realistic, and would still be a stretch for this employee.

Realistic goals eliminate compromises down the road. If you find
yourself willing to compromise the goal as time goes by, it was

probably too high (and unrealistic) to begin with. Beware of any goal that demands perfection. Perfection may be the ultimate objective, but seldom is it a realistic expectation.

Step 9. Use SMART to define each employee's responsibilities with goals that are TIME-BOUND.

The Reasons

Time-Bound. Specific goals clarify the "what" of the goal. Measurable goals clarify the "how much" or "how well" of the goal. Time-bound goals clarify the "when" of the goal. You don't end up complaining, "Clearly you should have done this by now!" Nor will your employees tell you, "I've had so many other things to do, this just kept slipping in favor of other priorities. But don't worry, I'll get it done soon."

Use time-bound goals to prevent procrastination from getting in the way of your employees' success. Use them to help you monitor and gauge progress and stay on track. Use them to tell you when it's time to hold an employee accountable.

The Basics

1. Start with a goal, stated as loosely as you like.
2. Ask, "What day or time, exactly, does this need to be done? What other work is dependent on this work? If this work goes undone, when would others notice or be negatively affected? If this task is done repeatedly, how much time (in minutes or days) should elapse between each time the task is done?"
3. Keep asking these questions.
4. Ask these questions over and over until you arrive at an actual date, time, or clearly defined frequency interval.

Start with a goal, loosely stated: "Get quarterly production results to line managers ASAP each quarter."

When, exactly, does this need to be done?
As soon as possible after the quarter ends.

What day or time?
*Usually the first or second week of the month after the quarter
is over.*

If this work goes undone, when will others notice or be negatively affected?
*Probably about the tenth or so of the month following the end
of the quarter.*

The original goal can be restated as "Get quarterly production
results to line managers within ten days of the quarter's end."

The Details

*To be time-bound, a goal must have a deadline (date) or frequency
level.* Again, the idea is to be able to quantify expectations.

- Complete Project XYZ by November 8.
- Vacuum the front lobby daily.
- Wipe the equipment down after every use.

But most managers use vague deadlines or frequency levels.
They assume employees know how important a goal is so that they
will do it soon enough or often enough. For instance:

"Clean the restroom often."
    How often is "often"? Does it mean every other day? Does
it mean every week? Does it mean every ten minutes, or after
anyone uses it?

*Time-bound goals remove ambiguity of when a goal should be ac-
complished.* Accountability is more clearly defined. When con-

fronted with a restroom that has not been cleaned in a while, an employee could rightfully argue, "I just cleaned it last night, and then again this morning. Isn't that enough?" Apparently, the goal's priority was not clear; that is not at all what you meant by "often." Help clarify the situation for yourself and your employee by saying, "Considering how often people go in there, we probably need it cleaned more frequently. Several times a day wouldn't be too much . . ."

A goal such as "Clean the restrooms every hour" is time-bound. Your employee either did or did not clean the restrooms every hour today. You could be talking about that measurable time frame instead of arguing about the definition of "often."

Don't put yourself in the position of clarifying your intentions after the fact. Avoid a confrontation and have that discussion now. Before it becomes an issue with your employees, make sure they understand up front when something should be done. Words like *regularly, frequently, often, consistently,* and *repeatedly* are frequently (pun intended) open to interpretation. Let them know exactly how often you want something done, or by what exact date. Does "third quarter" mean anytime during the third quarter, or by the start of third quarter, or by the last day of the third quarter? Be clear so you avoid assumptions or guesswork.

Frequency isn't always so obvious. Sometimes you will need to clarify a frequency level based on conditions other than clock or calendar time. For example:

"Restock clothing as necessary."

When should this be done? The answer depends on what makes restocking the clothing necessary in your mind. In this case, you must spell out for the employee when that is—what has to happen for it to be necessary.

Ask yourself, "What has to happen for this task to be necessary? What conditions must be present for the employee to engage? How will the employee know when she should do this task?" For instance:

"Restock clothing as necessary."

What has to happen for this task to be necessary?
The holding rack is over half full of clothes that need to be restocked.

How will the employee know it's time to do this task?
When her other tasks are done.

So the original goal could be restated with conditions that tell the employee when to do the task: "Restock clothing when the holding rack is half full and when your other tasks are completed."

A goal like this eliminates misunderstandings and clearly communicates expectations. Specify a time frame for your goals so that your employees' priorities match your own.

Checklist: Set Expectations

- ❏ I understand what my organization wants to accomplish by having reviewed its mission, vision, values, and strategies.
- ❏ I know what part of my organization's success is my team's responsibility, and I wholeheartedly accept that responsibility.
- ❏ I know what I will hold each of my employees responsible for. All of their individual responsibilities add up to the whole of what our team is collectively responsible for.
- ❏ My employees are either writing their own goals, or they are significantly helping me write them in the SMART format.
- ❏ Each goal is Specific. They are all clear, unambiguous, and focused. I've avoided labels and generalizations.
- ❏ Each goal is Measurable. I can count what I expect for each goal. I've avoided measures that are subjective and vague.
- ❏ Each goal is Action-oriented. They focus on behaviors, actions, and results. I've avoided trying to measure attitudes and intentions.

❑ Each goal is Realistic. My employees and I believe they can each be achieved in the time frame given. I've avoided asking for perfection and the unattainable.

❑ It is Realistic to expect all the goals together to be achieved in the time frame given.

❑ Each goal is Time-bound. I know when each must be completed. I've avoided making assumptions about priorities and urgencies.

CHAPTER 2

✓Invite Commitment

Your objective when you invite commitment is to get your employees to buy in to the goals so strongly that they truly want to accomplish them. When they want to reach a goal, they will welcome your holding them accountable for those results!

Employees will be best motivated to achieve results when they are clear on three things: what the goals are, why the goals exist, and most important, what's in it for them if they achieve the goals.

There should be no question in your mind what you are expecting of your employees, how much or what quality, and when. This was all covered by the SMART goals you developed in Chapter 1.

Step 1. Be prepared to explain to your employees why their goals exist.

The Reasons

Employees deserve to feel they are a part of something bigger than their own jobs. They will be more motivated and make better decisions when they understand how they fit in with the bigger picture. Connecting their SMART goals to the organization's direction gives meaning and purpose to those goals. Employees rally behind meaning and purpose with more resolve than they would to mere edicts or demands.

Employees want to know why they are doing something. They engage better when they understand and buy in to the reasons for doing it. Part of what will motivate your employees to success is knowing that they contribute to something worthwhile. Leverage that desire by checking that their goals support your organization's direction.

The Basics

1. Make sure that you can relate each goal to your organization's mission, vision, values, or strategy. If the goals don't tie in, consider whether you even have the right goals.
2. You should be able to explain the connection so that your employees readily see it. It should be crystal clear how their efforts will support your organization's direction.
3. You can even practice what you will say aloud so you can comfortably show how their goals relate to the bigger picture.

The Details

Keep these points in mind when explaining the goals to your employees.

If it's not clear to you, it will never be clear to them. So get clear now. Follow your line of reasoning from Chapter 1. Remember, your organization's mission, vision, strategies, and values drive the organization's goals. Organizational goals drive your team's goals. Team goals drive your employees' SMART goals. Follow that line backward and you'll have the link from individual contribution to big-picture success.

Know your employees. This is the key to using organizational reasons to engage your employees. You should be able to stress the organizational reasons that they will identify with most. You don't have to list every one. Emphasize those that best align with the employees' personal values or aspirations.

Step 2. Be prepared to explain to your employees what is in it for them if they reach their goals successfully.

The Reasons

Knowing what the goals are only makes it *possible* for your employees to succeed. Understanding why the goals exist only makes it *logical* for your employees to succeed. It's their own personal motivation that determines if your employees actually *will* succeed or not. Their biggest motivator is how they believe that they will be personally affected by the outcome of their actions and behaviors.

When employees believe it is in their own best interest to perform, they will. They will not perform when they believe it will harm them. They will not perform when they do not believe the promises held before them are real or attainable.

As you discuss goals, your employees will silently be asking themselves, "What's in it for me to do this?" The more you can answer that unarticulated question, the more likely you will engage your employees. Be able to answer that question for each and every goal and you're on your way to sure success!

The Basics

1. Know which *natural consequences* will appeal to your employees the most.
2. Highlight the *incentives* that the organization offers for meeting the goals.
3. Create individualized *incentives* if appropriate.
4. Use *negative threats* only as a last resort, or if mandated by your organization's policy.

The Details

Natural consequences. These are the natural results of a behavior or action. Although you usually can't control these, you may be able to augment or minimize them. At the very least, you can call them out for your employee to see, recognize, and value, as in the example below.

> Your employee's goal is "Complete Project ABC by June 29."
> Natural personal consequences for achieving this goal could include a sense of accomplishment, time in July freed up for other purposes, feeling good about meeting a deadline, exhilaration at having risen to a challenge, and an exposure to the budgeting process. You may be able to augment his exposure to the budgeting process by tweaking the project somehow to expand that element of the project. If you know the employee really values meeting deadlines, call that one out for him: "I know how important it is for you to meet all your deadlines. You pride yourself on that, and rightly so. I'm confident this will be another opportunity for you to demonstrate that value and demonstrate your passion for meeting your commitments!"

Be aware that there may also be natural consequences that are not valued by the employee. These may conflict directly with those that she values. Your employee will weigh the consequences and act accordingly, as in this situation:

> The employee's goal is "Complete Project ABC by June 29."
> Natural personal consequences for achieving this goal may include greater expectations for the next project, having to confront team members who are not performing their responsibilities on time, resentment from others who are not finishing their projects on time, or having to move from the known (this project) to the less comfortable unknown (the next project). Any of these natural consequences may discourage the employee from meeting the goal.

Natural consequences for *not* achieving a goal can motivate as well. If they are desirable, they will motivate your employee to not reach that goal:

> The employee's goal is "Complete Project ABC by June 29."
> Natural personal consequences for not accomplishing the goal

might include your having to lighten her workload in July so she can finish this project, lower expectations or demands for the next project, more attention and interaction with you or others during the crunch time, or more resources allocated to her to finish the project quickly. Any of these natural consequences could motivate the employee not to meet the goal.

By the same token, there may be natural consequences for *not* achieving the goal that may motivate the employee to actually achieve it:

The employee's goal is "Complete Project ABC by June 29." Natural personal consequences for not accomplishing the goal might include disapproval from senior management, an unmanageable workload in July, reduced respect from project team members, feelings of failure, or embarrassment at not having met a deadline. If this employee seeks upward career movement, he will especially want to avoid disappointing senior management.

The key to leveraging natural consequences is to know your employees well enough to emphasize the consequences that will most interest and encourage them. Be able to call out the natural consequences that will most appeal to them and motivate them.

Incentives. These are the consequences imposed by an outside party (you or your organization) for behavior or actions. You have much more influence or control over these results than you do over natural consequences, as shown below.

The employee's goal is "Complete Project ABC by June 29." Incentives may include public (or private) recognition and appreciation, an Employee of the Month award, a designated parking space, a sought-after next assignment, a box of candy, or even a cash bonus.

Just because you control or influence these results doesn't mean they are easy to manage. For example, the incentives may not be things that your employee values highly. Nor does she despise them. Employees will not be motivated by incentives they view as neutral:

> The employee's goal is "Complete Project ABC by June 29."
> You may have implemented incentives that include a framed certificate of completion and appreciation, tickets to the opera, an e-mail from the organization's top leader, and a company paperweight. Your employee may see these as marginal rewards, not worth her efforts to achieve the goal. If so, she will rely on other motivators to drive her effort, and these incentives are wasted on this particular employee.

One final point: Your incentives may include things that your employee wants to avoid. If so, they will have the opposite effect of the one you wanted, as in this example:

> The employee's goal is "Complete Project ABC by June 29."
> You may have implemented incentives that include public recognition of a project well done at the next staff meeting, the employee's picture in the company newsletter, lunch with senior management to celebrate, and a letter of recognition posted in the lunchroom. Your employee may dislike public fanfare. If he shies away from attention, these incentives may backfire. They may even drive him not to accomplish the goal just to avoid the negatively perceived incentives.

◆ *Do not underestimate the power of intangible incentives.* Just telling your employee that your team is counting on her may be a strong motivator. Your employee may value being part of a team effort, seeking the acceptance or approval of the team, or just feeling important.

By the same token, your personal charisma may come into play as well. Your employee may be motivated by a desire to impress you, get your approval, or just help you out. Leverage what makes each individual employee feel motivated.

◆ *Some incentives may be automatic or generic across your organization.* Take advantage of your organization's incentive programs, bonus policies, and recognition programs. Learn how your organization's incentives work so you can maximize their effectiveness with your employees. Learn who on your team is motivated by what and steer each person toward the applicable incentive.

Even if your organization has enterprisewide incentives, you'll usually still have some authority to create incentives that cost little but mean a great deal to your employees. Be creative and find things that you can provide that your employees would value. Check with upper management first, especially if you have a union contract or other employee agreements in place.

◆ *When all else fails, throw money at them, right?* Wrong. Do not assume that money is the ultimate incentive. Yes, it motivates many people in many situations. But it usually takes more than is in your budget. Countless other incentives that you can implement cost little to nothing, and they motivate stronger than cash ever will.

So what does motivate them? Each individual is different. This is where your expertise as a manager comes into play. The same things that motivate you will not necessarily motivate them. Find out was does motivate them—each of them. Use your own knowledge of each employee to determine what will appeal to him. Often, the natural consequences are enough. Create new incentives only when the natural consequences won't do it for them.

◆ *If you are not sure what will motivate, just ask.* Does that open a can of worms? It depends on how you ask:

"I want to motivate you to complete Project ABC by March 2. What will it take?" Or, "What can I offer you to get this done on time?" Instantly, you will be put into a position of saying no, as the responses could run the gamut. You don't want that. Instead, try: "I want you to be motivated to complete Project ABC. What will be the sticking points? Is there anything I can do to help you get past those points so you can hit the target?"

Or, "How would you like to celebrate when you finish this project on time?"

Simply opening this dialogue with employees begins to motivate them. They start to realize you are interested in helping them get what is important to them. You build trust. When they believe you are on their side, they are more likely to collaborate with you and, ultimately, get the job done via the goals you've defined for them.

Negative threats. You may be tempted to try to motivate your employees with the threat of negative consequences or incentives for not meeting their goals. This approach is rarely effective even for short-term results, and never effective in the long run. Except in rare cases, avoid this technique.

Idle threats are exposed quickly. Trust is lost when the manager is seen as someone who does not keep his or her word.

Strong performers have little patience for negative consequences. In time, they find other positions where the incentives are more in line with their value systems. This leaves the lower performers. Unable to find other positions, they often sabotage their own success or resist the goals indirectly. Still, there are sometimes reasons for going this route.

◆ *The manager has no positive incentives to offer.* The only natural consequences that apply seem to be negative ones that the employee should want to avoid. See what happens in this circumstance:

> Your employee's goal is "Balance your cash drawer every day without being more than one dollar over or under." You may not want to offer an incentive, and you may think that the temptation to steal is greater than the natural consequences. You may be missing positive natural consequences like a sense of pride in accurately conducting the day's business or the thrill of being "perfect" each day. In this case, you may threaten to punish employees who don't balance by putting them on a less desirable task or docking their pay. Fear of punishment may work temporarily, but eventually the fear will lose its power as honest

employees leave and dishonest employees find a way around the system you've created.

When there seem to be no positive reasons to reach a goal, look harder. Certainly there are compelling organizational reasons to call upon. These may be enough (not for all the goals, but for one or two goals in the context of the rest of the goals). You are probably missing some natural consequences. Dig deeper. What will happen if they do what you want them to do? What else? Why should they want to do it? Find the positive reasons to reach the goal.

◆ *The positive approach isn't working.* When the organizational reasons and personal reasons are not working, it's because the employee hasn't bought into them.

Your employee's goal is "Balance your cash drawer every day without being more than one dollar over or under." Several organizational reasons, incentives, and natural consequences are used unsuccessfully. In frustration you may impose a threat to dock pay or reassign employees who don't balance their cash drawers. Again, this fear of punishment may work temporarily, but the decent employees will soon leave, and the dishonest ones will find ways to thwart your efforts.

Somehow you missed what truly motivates this employee. Consider also what he is getting (natural consequences) by not performing. As a last resort, consider whether this employee is a good fit for this job at all. Perhaps a mismatch needs to be corrected.

◆ *The only time negative threats might be used appropriately is for an employee who faces disciplinary action.* If your organization uses negative incentives, it's only fair to let your employees know about them up front.

Your employee's goal is "Balance your cash drawer every day without being more than one dollar over or under." The employee was out of balance today. The next time she is out of balance, she will be given a disciplinary letter. It is proper to

give the employee fair warning about what "negative incentive"
she may incur if she continues not to meet expectations. Or, tell
her if your company has a policy of terminating employees who
are out of balance more than $100.

If an employee is in the disciplinary process, let him know what
the next step may be if you need to take that action (more on this
in Chapter 5). You won't want to rely exclusively on these negative
incentives, though. Balance them heavily with the more positive
reasons—both organizational and personal.

The SMART goals tell employees specifically what is expected.
The organizational reasons tell employees why this is expected. The
personal reasons help employees see why they personally should
engage. All three components are critical. With all three in place,
your employees will want to accomplish their goals. They will want
to be successful. They will even want to be held accountable!

Step 3. Get ready for your discussion about goals with your employees.

The Reasons

Like anything else, the more prepared you are for a discussion with
your employees about goals, the more likely your success. You can
anticipate objections or other sticking points and plan for resolution up front. But most of all, if you are prepared, you'll feel more
confident as you go into the discussion.

By now, you have the SMART goals that were derived from
your organization's overall direction. You are able to speak to the
organizational and personal reasons why employees should engage.
There are a few more basics to cover before you're ready to ask your
employees to commit to the goals.

The Basics

1. Resolve any concerns you may have with the goals yourself.

2. Anticipate how your employees may react and plan accordingly.
3. Create the environment that will encourage and support this kind of conversation.

The Details

Resolve your own concerns with the goals. Make sure that you are on board with these expectations before you try to get your employees on board.

Why do you need to be on board? You will not be able to convince the employees of the goals if you are not convinced yourself. Your own lack of commitment will come across in your tone, your body language, and in your attitude. Your belief in what you are asking them to do will come across in the way you present it.

If you have any reservations, double-check to be sure each goal is realistic. Once you are confident that each goal is realistic, look again. But this time look at all the goals together. Is it realistic to expect one person to do all of them within the time frames you've outlined? You need to be confident that your employees can achieve all that you are expecting of them. If you don't believe it, now is the time to resolve it. Revise the goals, or get help from a peer or your own boss. Don't approach your employees until you've bought in yourself.

Anticipate employee reactions and plan accordingly. You can better deal with objections if you are prepared for them.

You know your employees. You can predict with some accuracy how they will react to the goals. If you expect a negative reaction, get ready for it now.

Anticipate how your employees will react to each goal, and to all of them together. What will they be most excited about? What will they resist the most? How strongly will they resist it? Why will they resist it? Use this information to plan how you deliver the goals. It may change the order in which you reveal them. It may affect the level of detail you go into for each one. You may want to start with what you expect employees' objections to be and address them right up front. Or wait for the objection, but be confident in your readiness to respond appropriately.

Consider how your employees may try to get around a goal. How could they fulfill the mechanics of the goal (and thus meet it) but still miss the point of the goal (the real intent)? In this case, the individual may win while the organization loses. What are the "loopholes" in the goal, and should they be closed up? Here's an example:

> The goal is "Every table is wiped down after every customer." An employee may wipe all the tables down with a single, barely damp rag. After a few tables, the rag itself is dirty. The rest of the tables will still get wiped down but with the dirty rag. They will still be dirty. Your employee met the goal as it was stated but got around the real intent: a clean table for the next customer. "Every table is clean enough to eat off of for each new customer" may be a better way to state the same goal and get at the real purpose.

Have a practice run-through with a trusted friend or colleague. Hear yourself saying the words and assess how you come across. Ask your partner to respond the way you expect your employees to react.

There is nothing wrong with using notes when you need them. Better to use notes than make big mistakes that you regret later.

Set up the environment so it is conducive for an important, serious discussion. Plan on having this discussion in a quiet, private place where you won't be interrupted. Make sure you have enough time scheduled to spend on this important discussion. If your employees see you taking this seriously, they are more apt to do the same.

If possible, set an appointment with your employees in advance, rather than just springing this on them. Let them prepare mentally and emotionally for this discussion just as you do. If they will have input into their goals, this lead time allows them to do their prep work. If they don't have input, consider sharing the goals with them beforehand so they can come prepared with questions.

This conversation sets you up to hold your employees accountable. You can't afford to do anything less than give it your best. Spend the time and energy up front to get ready and be prepared for success.

Step 4. Present or discuss the goals with your employees.

The Reasons

It is now time to discuss the goals with your employees and invite them to commit to attaining them. You are more likely to meet with success if they want to reach the goals than if they are merely compelled to do so. To fully engage, they need to understand two things: the specifics of the goals within the context of the big picture and what's in it for them if they succeed.

This discussion will prepare them to make a commitment to achieve the goals.

The Basics

1. Put your employees' goals into the context of the bigger picture. Make sure they understand how they fit in and how they will contribute to a greater whole.
2. Discuss each goal in detail. Together, explore all aspects of each goal. Make sure you all completely understand a goal before moving on to the next one.
3. Help your employees see what is in it for them personally to achieve the goals. They need to see how it is in their own best interest to get on board with the goals.
4. Handle their reaction to the goals. Help them come to terms with the goals and to understand them well enough to commit to achieving them.
5. Welcome employee questions and concerns.

The Details

Put your employees' goals into context. Share your organization's mission, vision, strategies, or values. Show how your organization's direction is driving what your team is required to do. Explain how your employees' roles fit in with those of other team members to get the job done. Help them see how doing their job well and meeting their goals will ultimately contribute toward the organization's overall mission and vision.

Discuss each goal in detail. You should be able to link each goal to the bigger picture, as done below:

> "Our competitor's average call wait time is only 63 seconds. If we are to remain competitive, we must get ours under one minute this year. To make this happen, your goal for handling calls will be to take 8.4 calls per hour."
>
> Not only does the employee know what is expected (8.4 calls per hour) but why it is expected (an effort to close in on the competition).

Stay focused and stick to the facts. You'll lose your employees if you start to ramble, go off on tangents, or jump from goal to goal. You may even get confused or lost yourself. (Again, bring notes if you need them.) It is critical that your employees know exactly what is expected of them. Simple, uncomplicated data is best here.

Tell your employees what's in it for them if they reach their goals. This is the real draw for your employees. Sure, they care about the organization, but they care more intensely about their own circumstances. Show them how meeting their goals will benefit them personally. Not only will they agree to those goals, but they will also commit to them. Commitment is preferable to compliance.

There is something that gives most employees a buzz when they do their job well. Perhaps it's the feeling they get when they hear the applause after a presentation, or when they see the criminal sent to jail, or when they feel a trusting child take their hand. Whatever it is, it's internal. It drives their action more strongly than incentives. Learn what this is for each employee:

> "Our competitor's average call wait time is only 63 seconds. If we are to remain competitive, we must get ours under one minute this year. To this end, your goal for handling calls will be to take 8.4 calls per hour."
>
> For the employee whom you know relishes competition and the thrill of beating her old employer, you may add, "Imagine how good you will feel when you know you are beating those guys!" Or, for the employee whom you know is motivated by public recognition, you may add, "Each week you average 8.4 calls or better, your name will be posted and we'll recognize you at the staff meeting." And for the employee whom you know is inspired by helping others, you could add, "Think about all the extra people you personally will be able to help each week if you average 8.4 calls per hour!"

The organizational reasons for the goal explain why the goal exists but not necessarily why an employee should make an effort to accomplish it. Personal reasons—natural consequences and incentives that really matter—will convince your employees that they want to engage. And when they want to accomplish the goals, they are much more receptive to being held accountable for those results. They will view accountability as your way of helping them get what they want.

Ask for their reaction to the goals. Find out directly rather than guessing or inferring:

> How do you feel about this? What do you think of that? What's your reaction to this goal? What clarity do you need? Will you be able to accomplish it? How confident are you about this goal?

It may be tempting to just plow through all the goals at once and then ask for any questions at the end. While this makes it easier for you, it encourages all of you to gloss over details and leads to misunderstanding. Your employees may forget questions that arise as new goals are thrown at them. Make sure they understand each goal completely before going on to the next one.

Welcome their questions and concerns. It's always better to hash things out now, when it's easier to stay rational and objective, than later, when emotions run high during a crisis. Remember, your employees wouldn't be asking questions if they didn't care. Apathy and indifference are more difficult to deal with and harder to turn around than resistance.

Answer their questions fully and completely. This is not the time to watch the clock or skim over details. The better the understanding now, the less trouble you'll have later.

If they don't have any questions, ask some more yourself to check their understanding. You may see their quietness or immediate acceptance of the goals as good signs. This may or may not be so. Beware the employee who will mildly accept any goal just to get out of the meeting with you, and then go out and not work toward the goals you just discussed.

Step 5. Seek buy-in or commitment to the goals.

The Reasons

You have explained the context of your employees' goals to them. They know precisely what is expected of them. They understand how their efforts fit into the big picture. They appreciate how reaching their goals will help the organization meet its objectives. And most important, they see how reaching their goals will benefit them personally.

Your employees will now have one of four responses toward their goals: buy-in, commitment, acceptance, or rejection. Do not settle for rejection or even mere acceptance of the goal without commitment. Neither allows you to hold your employees accountable.

Buy-in is best. Your employee makes the goals his or her own. Commitment is also good. Your employee commits to doing what it will take to reach the goals. With either, you pass the point of no return; both responses set you up for full accountability.

Remember, your employees are more likely to buy in or commit to the goals if they have had a hand in creating them.

The Basics

1. Ask your employees to buy in to the goals:

   - "Can you make these goals your own?"
   - "Which of these goals do you already feel are personal for you?"
   - "Which goals get you most excited?"

2. If your employees don't buy in, ask them to commit to the goals:

   - "Will you commit to achieving all of these goals?"
   - "Will you work to accomplish each and every goal?"
   - "Can I count on you to achieve all of this?"

3. Do not allow your employees to reject or merely accept the goals. Neither of these responses will permit you to hold them accountable.

4. Once your employees buy in or commit, discuss briefly how they might go about attaining the goals. This discussion will help you determine if they really understand what they are getting into.

The Details

Rejection. Your employees refuse the goals. They probably see the goals as either unrealistic or unfair compared to what's expected of others. If they are bold enough to reject the goals, they will likely say so directly, as in:

- "No, I won't be able to do all that."
- "Hmm, that sure is different from what everyone in Benjamin's group is expected to do."

- "I don't think so; that's too much to ask. How about if I do this much instead?"

◆ *Don't take their rejection or resistance personally.* Remember, it's better to deal with resistance than with apathy. If they're resistant, at least they care enough to spend energy standing up to you. Help redirect that energy toward a solution that works for all of you. Find out where the sticking point is and resolve it together. You may have to go back over each goal one at a time or check the goals as a whole.

Strong resistance is often a signal that your employees see the goals as unrealistic or that you have not addressed what's in it for them. Check your assumptions. How will these employees win or benefit when they accomplish these goals?

As a last resort, consider whether a particular resistant person is a right fit for the job. Perhaps he or she is better suited for other work.

◆ *Stand firm.* Reinforce that the goals must be met, and then explore ways to meet them. Look at the example below.

> "Chris, the goals are set. They must get done. What we can do is look into different ways of how you can achieve them. What are some of the options before us?"
>
> Then discuss different ideas for how the goals can be met realistically.

With the goals on the table, emphasize the need to meet them. Decide beforehand whether you will allow yourself to be put in a position of negotiating expectations. Unless there is room for negotiation, these goals are set.

Acceptance. Your employees receive the goals without promising to accomplish them. You are more likely to hear an acceptance than a flat-out rejection. You may hear things like:

- "Well, I will try."
- "I'll do my best."

- "Is that everything? It's worth a shot."
- "I can't make any promises, but I'll sure give it my all."

If your employees don't commit to accomplishing the goals, you will have difficulty holding them accountable. It's nearly impossible to hold people accountable for "trying" or "doing their best." How would you measure trying? How would you know if they did their best? Look at the next scenario.

Employee: "Yeah, sure, these goals look okay."
Manager: "Will you accomplish them?"
Employee: "Well, I'll certainly do my best, you know that!"
Manager: "Great, I know I can count on you to do your best. Will you commit to reaching each of these goals?"
Employee: "I'll try my hardest to meet them, okay?"

For this employee, pledging his best efforts leaves him an "out" if he fails. It will be difficult to hold him accountable later if all you had was his "I'll try!"

◆ *Your employees may be hedging.* They may realize that if they commit to meeting these goals, you will be able to hold them accountable. Some employees may want to resist that:

"I said I'd do my best, what more do you want than that? I'll try my hardest to meet them, okay?"

"What I need is a commitment from you that you will not just try but actually reach each of the goals. Can I count on you to try hard, *and* to deliver?"

This employee may just need some encouragement and support. If so, a direct request will flush that out, and you can then encourage or support her.

◆ *Your employees may be rejecting indirectly.* They say they want to try or work hard, but they really disagree with the goals and are unwilling to state that directly:

Employee: "These goals look fine."
Manager: "Will you accomplish them?"
Employee: "Well, I'll do the best that I can."
Manager: "Great, I know I can count on you to do your best. Will you commit to reaching each of these goals?"
Employee: "I said I'd do my best, so I'll try my hardest to meet them, all right?"
Manager: "What I need you to do is to try hard and to achieve the goals. Will you commit to doing that?"
Employee: "I don't know if I can."

If your employee doesn't commit now, he is probably rejecting. Check by asking directly, "Are these goals unattainable?" Get it out in the open and you can deal directly and constructively with the rejection.

Commitment. Your employees promise to achieve their goals. This is the minimal response that allows you to hold your employees accountable for results. Do not settle for anything less. Without it, you are headed for trouble.

Ask your employees directly to commit to reaching the goals. Accept only a direct answer. Anything less than an explicit "yes" is either a rejection or mere acceptance (see above). Some people don't distinguish between pledging their best and committing to reach a goal. For them, it's a matter of semantics. For others the two are completely different. Assume the latter and always work with them until you get a clear commitment—a promise to accomplish the goal:

Employee: "These goals look pretty good."
Manager: "Will you accomplish them?"
Employee: "You know I'll try my hardest."
Manager: "Great, I know I can count on you to work hard. Will you commit to reaching each of these goals?"
Employee: "Yeah, sure."

Buy-in. Your employees promise to achieve the goals, and they make those goals their own. They internalize the goals and they resolve to do whatever it takes to be successful. This is the ultimate. When employees buy in, they are more apt to work harder and look for ways to be successful. They are less likely to accept failure, to blame others, or to look for excuses.

Employees will *commit* to goals when they understand them, agree that they are realistic, and see the connection between their goals and the organization's direction. However, employees will *buy in* to goals when they also believe that by accomplishing those goals, they will benefit personally. They see what's in it for them. They realize that when they achieve their goals, they win personally as well as professionally.

Buy-in allows them to keep themselves motivated and even hold *themselves* accountable. It prompts them to overcome obstacles and disappointments. It encourages them to solve problems and make good decisions. It makes them want to be held accountable for results, because they stand to personally benefit.

Before going further, make sure you have explicit buy-in or at least a commitment for the goals. Without one of those, it's impractical to go forward.

Step 6. Document their agreement to meet their goals in a Performance Plan.

The Reasons

To hold someone accountable for results, both employer and employee have to remember the commitments clearly and plainly. People's memories are often fuzzy. Jotting down notes may help, but simple notes may lose the clarity of your goals. Take advantage of the sureness that a Performance Plan offers.

A Performance Plan is simply a record of your employees' agreement to reach their goals. You will use it to remind them of their commitments and to hold them accountable. They will use it to remember what they've committed to, what they're responsible for accomplishing, and to keep themselves from veering from what's most important.

The Basics

1. Record each goal in the SMART goal format.
2. Record any adjustments, allowances, contingencies, or other modifications you discussed and agreed to.
3. You and your employee each get a copy of the documentation.

The Details

Have your employees write up their own Performance Plans. By documenting their own commitments, your employees reinforce their own resolve.

Read their Performance Plan carefully. The finished document will give you a good sense of whether they really get it or not. Watch for wording that could be later misconstrued or even twisted to weaken the goal's intended impact.

The makeup of a Performance Plan. The plan consists of five distinct elements:

1. *General Identification.* This area records demographic information about whose Performance Plan this is. It often contains the employee's name, her formal job title and grade, employee ID number, the manager's name, and the time frame covered by the Performance Plan. It may also include a schedule for when the manager and employee will meet for progress reports and accountability.
2. *Major Areas of Responsibility.* This area breaks the employee's job responsibilities into large overall areas to be covered by his goals.
3. *SMART Goals.* This area lists each and every goal in SMART format.
4. *Support or Resources Provided by the Manager.* This area lists what role you will play in helping your employee to successfully meet her goals.
5. *Signatures.* Both employee and manager sign in agreement of the Performance Plan.

The Performance Plan should be a working document. As the organization's needs change, you and your employee may need to adjust expectations. If goals are altered, deleted, or added, they should be recorded accordingly so the Performance Plan is always current and relevant.

EXAMPLE: Performance Plan

Name: Chris Employee

Position: Sales Support Assistant

Department: THC Sales Group

Time frame: Jan 1–Dec 31

Manager: Lynn Manager

PERFORMANCE GOALS

Major Area of Responsibility #1:
Receptionist for the THC Sales Group: greeting/guiding customers and other department visitors, responding to and directing customer and internal telephone calls, handling internal/external mail.

SMART Goals:
- Answer all incoming calls on or before the fourth ring.
- Direct calls to the appropriate contact on the first try, every time.
- Take accurate and complete messages and ensure delivery of all messages to the appropriate party within two hours.
- Greet visitors as soon as they arrive. Direct them to the appropriate area or person immediately.
- Make sure the receptionist desk and phones are covered at all times.
- Sort and deliver all incoming mail and correspondence within two hours of receipt.

Major Area of Responsibility #2:
Maintaining the department filing system.

SMART Goals:
- File all policy and other manual updates accurately and within one week of receipt.
- File all correspondence accurately within two days of receipt.
- File Project: Clean the customer and vendor files by April 30—create files for new customers and vendors, purge old files, and update existing files.

Major Area of Responsibility #3:
Word processing: creating documents and slide presentations, typing correspondence, creating spreadsheets, etc.

SMART Goals:
- Complete all routine correspondence and other non-project-related typing within twenty-four hours unless otherwise specified at the time of receipt.
- All typing and data input will be free of errors.
- Assist with projects (including budget preparation) by providing typing, charts, graphs, slides, etc. per the project timelines and quality requirements.
- Input all HR-related data into the system within three days of receipt.

Major Area of Responsibility #4:
Scheduling and coordination of conference rooms, meetings, and travel arrangements for the THC Sales Group.

SMART Goals:
- Schedule conference room 4D so that there are never overlapping conflicts.
- Clean conference room 4D after each meeting—no trash anywhere, chairs arranged neatly around the table, flip-chart paper off the walls, trash cans emptied, and tables cleared off completely.

- Coordinate travel arrangements for THC staff to minimize costs for air, hotel, and car rentals within two days of the request.
- Prepare agendas for the weekly staff meetings and distribute to all participants no less than twenty-four hours before the meeting.
- Take notes at weekly staff meetings, recording all agreements made as well as action items to be done, by whom, and by when. Distribute minutes within forty-eight hours of the meeting to all THC staff members.

Major Area of Responsibility #5:
Budget and invoice support.

SMART Goals:
- Invoices are processed on time—no penalties, late charges, or delinquent notices are ever received.
- Invoices are processed in time to take advantage of discounts, bank float, or other cost-saving measures (whenever such things are available).
- Monthly budget reports are reviewed within two weeks of receipt and the manager is notified of any variances and exceptions.

BEHAVIORAL GOALS

Customer Focus
- Conform to the dress code daily (see the employee handbook for details).
- Get the name of every department visitor and use it at least once in your interaction with him or her.

Initiative
- Implement way(s) to save yourself two hours per week on current administrative processes by the end of the year.
- Implement way(s) to save the organization at least $1,000 this year.

Teamwork

- Actively participate in all team meetings, team activities, and team decisions.
- Give positive recognition to a team member at least once a month—recognition must be specific and detailed.

Communications

- Bring rumors to the manager for clarification, rather than spreading them to anyone else.
- Do not share confidential information with others inappropriately.

Leadership

- Sign up to mentor at least one employee through the Mentoring Program.
- Take at least three initiatives that would be considered "risks" and debrief with your manager about the outcome of each.

MANAGER SUPPORT AND RESOURCES

1. Set expectation with Kerry to provide lunch and break coverage for phones and reception area by June 29.
2. By March 15, contract with a temp agency for a two-week assistant to cover during the File Project in mid-April.
3. Sign invoices and other approvals immediately, or if not possible, then within twenty-four hours of receipt.
4. Make computer-training class arrangements for PowerPoint by December 17.

Agreed to:

_____   _____

Employee   **Manager**

_____   _____

Date   **Date**

Checklist: Invite Commitment

- ❏ I can explain why my employees' goals exist. I can make the direct link between each goal and our organization's direction.
- ❏ I can show each employee what is in it for him personally if he achieves his goals.
- ❏ I understand what motivates each employee from within, and I am able to help her get that buzz from her own success.
- ❏ I have developed or plan to use incentives that I know will appeal to my employees' needs and wants (which may differ from my own).
- ❏ I have resolved any concerns I had about their goals.
- ❏ I am ready and eager to discuss goals with my employees in an environment that is conducive to such a discussion.
- ❏ I am ready for my employees' reactions to their goals, even if the reactions are negative. I am confident that I can get them to fully understand their goals.
- ❏ I am ready to ask my employees for buy-in or commitment to their goals. I will recognize their positive response when I hear it.
- ❏ I know how to turn an "acceptance" response to goals into a commitment.
- ❏ I am confident about handling any "rejection" response I may hear.
- ❏ I will have my employee document our discussion and agreement about goals in a Performance Plan.
- ❏ Each employee and I will keep a copy of the Performance Plan.
- ❏ We will revisit the Performance Plan periodically to keep it up-to-date and relevant.

CHAPTER 3

✓Measure Results

Some goals are easy to count—the time it takes to process an order, the number of widgets made, the amount of sales generated. Those goals have measures already built right in. Most goals, however, require you to build a measurement process or tool in order to track them. While anything *can* be measured, the key is to find a way to measure things effectively.

Step 1. Make sure the measurement tools you use are *efficient*.

The Reasons

Measurement can take on a life all its own and end up costing more than is necessary or prudent. You don't want measuring the goal to wipe out the benefits of your employee actually reaching that goal.

The Basics

Find measurement tools that minimize cost, time, and effort.

The Details

Spend less money on measurement tools and still get useful data. The best measurements do not have to cost a fortune to be effective. Look for options that get the job done inexpensively, as in the example below.

The goal for a personal trainer is "Help each client reach her or his personal fitness goals." To measure this, you could hire people to pose as clients and get feedback from them on how the personal trainer is doing the job. This could be effective, but very costly. Rather than go to that expense, you could randomly poll the personal trainer's clients for their candid assessments of his performance with them.

Get results back quickly. While you wait for the performance data, your employees may repeat undesirable behaviors. Intentional or not, they are justified in continuing their behavior until they are told otherwise. Make the measurement results available as quickly as possible. For instance:

The goal for a Web-based graphic artist is "Create eye-catching ads by April 27 that increase sales by 16 percent." It may take weeks, months, or even longer to find out if sales increased due to a new banner ad. Instead of waiting for those results, assume that more banner hits will translate into more sales. Count the number of hits on the new banner ads.

Make the tracking process effortless for everyone. The easier it is to track progress, the better. The more effort it takes, the more likely it is that you'll stop using that method for tracking. Make measurement as effortless as possible for you and your employees:

The goal for a groundskeeper is "No grass clippings left on client's driveway or sidewalk after mowing." To measure this, you could travel behind your crews and check each property they service to make sure no grass clippings are left on the driveway or sidewalk. This would require great effort (and time!) on your part. Another approach might be to give each crew an inexpensive digital camera. Have them photograph each property from two different angles after they are done. Require that each picture show the driveway and sidewalks with the lawn to show the picture was taken after their work was done.

Don't track everything just because you can. You do not need to track every move your employees make. Simply measure results to determine if your employees are following through on their commitments. Use measurement tools to track only the key indicators of progress, or you'll end up wasting time, money, and effort:

> The goal for a maid is "No visible dust left on any horizontal surface in a home." To measure this, you could check each and every horizontal surface in the home that was just cleaned by your employee. This would be time-consuming and not turn up problems any better than a sampling would. Instead, randomly select one room in the house as a sample of the work done throughout. Check the horizontal surfaces there. Agree with your employee beforehand that it will be indicative of the type of work done elsewhere in the home.

Step 2. Make sure the measurement tools you use are *fair*.

The Reasons

Fair measurement tools encourage your employees to buy in to the measurement process more quickly and more fully. Fair measurement tools also earn you the trust and respect that you need to give feedback and otherwise hold your employees accountable.

The Basics

1. Find measurement tools that are fair and unbiased.
2. Find tools that measure what they are supposed to measure—no more, no less.

The Details

Measure the right stuff. Just because it's easy to measure or commonly measured elsewhere doesn't mean it's the right thing to measure. Track only what is truly relevant to your employee's performance and success. For example:

The goal for a teacher is "Get through the history-of-Ohio unit in three weeks or less." This goal suggests that the quicker he completes this unit, the better. Measuring how long it takes to get through the unit may not measure what is really important. In his effort to meet this goal, the teacher may rush discussion or even cut off questions altogether. This doesn't fit with the school's mission to give its students a well-rounded education. The real goal is to give students an understanding of the history of their state. It should be measured in ways other than how fast the material is covered. A better measurement would be the students' scores on a standardized history exam. If a time frame is important, add it.

Minimize intrusion. The more in-your-face you are, the more you might negatively influence your employees' behavior. They may resent your presence. They may feel nervous being watched and perform poorly because of it. Measurement tools should be able to track progress without getting in the way of your employees' getting their jobs done. Let's look at another example.

The goal for a customer service rep is "Use the caller's name at least three times during each call." You might measure this by sitting next to the employee and listening to each call for the use of names. This may intimidate your employee. She may behave differently just because you are watching or listening to her. Another option, if you have the resources, would be to record phone calls and listen to them at your convenience. The employee is more likely to act naturally when you are not omnipresent. Knowing that she is being recorded may still affect her behavior, but not as noticeably as when someone sits next to her, breathing over her shoulder.

Balance an employee's right to privacy with the level of information you need for each job. Some jobs may require more detail or have greater customer impact or higher legal liability and justify a tighter, closer measurement process.

Measure only what is within your employees' control. It's not fair to hold your employees accountable for something that is out of their control. Find what they do control and measure that. For example:

> The goal for a trainer is "Get an average score of 4.5 or better on training evaluations." The evaluations include questions about the registration process, the training facility, and the printed training manual. The trainer has no control over these things. The scores on those questions could affect his score in a way that does not reflect his actual performance delivering the training. Single out the questions that specifically relate to the way the class was conducted (pace, open discussions, and covering the material thoroughly), and use those as indicators of progress toward the goal.

Don't create measurement tools in a vacuum. While you may think you know how to measure, your employees may have some very good input on what could work even better. At least listen to them. Involve them in the process of deciding how to measure their goals. Those that have input are more likely to accept the measurement tool you use and thus accept the data from it more readily.

Step 3. Make sure the measurement tools you use are *simple*.

The Reasons

The more complicated the tracking process is, the more likely the focus will shift away from results and onto the measurement itself. Simple is better.

The Basics

1. Find measurement tools that are simple and unencumbered.
2. Automate the measurement process.

The Details

Use automatic measurement tools. Manual processes tend to be more cumbersome, require more effort, and are subject to more errors than automatic processes. They distract employees from their primary focus. They are time-consuming and lower employee morale. Automate whenever possible. You and your employees then can free up your time and energy to focus on what's really important: getting the job done well. For example:

> The goal for a data input operator is "Don't be late to start your shift more than twice a month." When your employee is late, she is required to report to you first. Then you log how late she arrived in a binder. But what if you're not near your binder? When you are not present, who will record it for you? What if your late employee forgets to report to you? There are too many opportunities for error. Perhaps a simple computer program can be written to log employees in and out as they sit at their workstation and make their first keystroke. Automate the tracking and it will be more accurate and objective.

Use exception reporting. Don't measure everyday routines. This is tedious and unnecessary. You can get the same indication of success by counting only the exceptions to the norm. To illustrate:

> The goal for a grocery store bagger is "Bag the groceries so that the customer is satisfied with the arrangement and the weight of each bag." You could ask each customer if she is satisfied. You could count the number of times a customer lifts the bag and walks away without comment. But this would happen constantly, and you would be doing a lot of counting. Exception counting would be easier and more efficient. Try "Bag the groceries so that you get fewer than two complaints per week from customers because of bag weight or how the items were packed." Counting only the exceptions to expected good performance has a negative focus. However, the time and effort it frees up usually excuses the negative slant.

Don't make it overly complicated. Keep it simple. Keep the focus on the job, not the measurement of the job. Even if the measurement tool is not perfect, the tradeoff is usually worth it, as shown in this example:

> The goal for a hairstylist is "Create original and beautiful styles for clients so that you get a tip of over 20 percent, or at least 15 percent, and a compliment to management, or a 10 percent tip and a positive comment card, or at least two referrals from the customer within two months." Although this goal is measurable, the complexity makes it difficult to track. A simpler way would be to merely count how many repeat customers the hair stylist has. If the style was original, creative, and well liked, the client will return. Repeat business will be simpler to count than the combination of tips and comments.

Step 4. Use and share the data as soon as it is available.

The Reasons

Waiting until the end of a reporting period may be too late for you to take corrective action if the work is not going well. Employees need information to improve their performance. Hoarding the data until you are ready to share it with your employees only delays improvement.

The Basics

1. Use and share the data with each employee immediately.
2. Share data with employees that will encourage healthy competition among them for better results.

The Details

Use measurement data as it becomes available. Don't wait until the end of a reporting period to act on your information. You may want to use interim goals or milestones that allow you to track progress on longer projects or tasks without having to wait until the end. For example:

The goal for a sales rep is "Increase market share 4 percent by year end." The goal is not truly met or missed until December 31. If you follow that logic, you will not measure it until that date. If the goal is missed, nothing can be done to save the year. You could break the goal up into smaller chunks (1 percent per quarter). Or there might be other tasks that linked to the goal that could be good milestones. Maybe four sales calls per day, six site visits per week, or two new customers per month would be good benchmarks. Anything that indicates real progress toward the ultimate goal of increasing market share by 4 percent that year could be used as an interim goal.

Share the data as soon as you get it. Why wait? The data should be available to both you and your employees right away. You may still need to have a discussion about the results. If you do, your employees need that data to prepare for the discussion. Even if you don't need to talk about it, your employees appreciate the immediate validation that they are on the right track. In either case, it's worth it to share the data immediately.

Promote competition. Sometimes, competition among co-workers can promote greater results. Use this tactic wisely. Beware those who give up easily as well as those who compete too fiercely. Keep individual names confidential. Competition-promoting tactics might include:

- Posting daily sales figures
- Allowing employees access to average call wait time for other units
- Distributing a monthly report on budget variances

Step 5. Implement the measurement tools and gather the data.

The Reasons
Tweaking measurement tools indefinitely will get you nowhere. At some point you have to declare a starting place and begin to mea-

sure the results so you have information to check your employees' progress toward their goals.

The Basics

1. If you have used a particular measurement tool before and it works well for you, keep using it.
2. If you will use a new tool, test it to be sure it measures what you want. Try it for a short time and then evaluate the results.
3. Express your confidence and trust in the measurement tools.
4. Start collecting data as soon as your employees commit to their goals. No need to wait unless their goals are tied to a specific time period that hasn't started yet.

The Details

Allow your employees access to the data. If there is a problem with the measurement tool, your employees will spot it immediately and you can correct it before more time is lost.

If the results are favorable, the data reinforces your employees' efforts and they are more apt to continue their good work. If results are unfavorable, your employees get an immediate message that something needs to change. They can start working on improvement even before you find time to discuss it with them.

Express your confidence in the measurement tools. Your employees will pick up on your cues. If you have faith in the measurement tools, so will they. Mutual trust and belief in the measurement tools helps you avoid arguments about "bad data."

Record the data. You may have to refer to the data more than once, so make sure it's documented somewhere. Record the data manually if it doesn't get recorded automatically. Don't rely on your memory to recall what did or did not happen.

Use discretion in determining whether to allow your employees to record their own results data. This will be a function of how serious the data is as well as how much you trust your employees personally. For instance:

- Have your employee keep a tally of how many times she takes a phone order each day.
- Do not have your employee track how much money she was over or under at the end of the day.

Compare any data collected in the past to the data you collect now to spot trends and patterns. Keep the data someplace convenient so you can find it when you need it.

Step 6. Compare the actual results you measured to the goals.

The Reasons

The raw data collected is almost useless without the goals. When you compare what your employees actually did (results) with what they were supposed to do (goals), you get information that means something. This is half of what you will eventually present to your employees when you give them feedback.

The Basics

Do a gap analysis of actual results to the goals.

The Details

Learn what to do with the data you've collected. How do the results compare to the goals you've set for your employees?

Compare the actual results to the goals. If your employees meet or exceed their goals, celebrate! Recognize those employees with positive feedback. If there is a gap between the expected results and the actual results, you will need to hold your employees accountable. Figure out what the gap is. Quantify it.

This is where all your hard work creating measurable goals starts to really pay off. The gap analysis is simple when the goals are so well defined and measured. If you struggle to articulate the gap between expected and actual results, consider your goals again. Are they truly SMART?

Understand the performance gap fully. Look at the data again; make sure the gap is legitimate before you take further action. Study the data so you are familiar with it well enough to discuss it in detail with your employees. You may want to use tools that help show the gap—a simple table or chart, a spreadsheet, a sample of the work, and so on.

You may use the results to establish performance review ratings. Data can be used to determine how performance ratings will be used in the performance review process. Data gathered might also be used as a benchmark for determining what to expect in the future.

Step 7. Identify the organization's gain or loss due to your employees' actions.

The Reasons

You need one more piece of information before you are ready to talk to your employees about their performance: the organizational impact. Telling your employees how their results compare to their goals will be half of the feedback you deliver. That is the "what" of your feedback. The "why" is the other half. The impact your employees' behavior has on the organization helps you make a case for them to change or improve.

The Basics

1. Look at the gap analysis from step 6.
2. Ask, "What is the direct result of my employees' actions? How are things different because of what they did? How much did this cost or save us? What is better or worse now because of what they did?"

The Details

Identify how your employees' actions affected the organization. Each employee's goals are linked back to the organization's direction. Collectively, the employees' performance cannot help but have some impact on the organization somewhere, somehow. They may have an effect on time, money, morale, customer satisfaction, quality, or some other factor.

When there is a performance gap, identify how what employees did (or did not do) affected the organization. It may have been lower customer satisfaction, higher cost, rework, scrap, time lost, or something else. Look at the example below:

> Your employee didn't clean his equipment before leaving for the day. The buildup of grime causes the equipment to run slower. Slower equipment creates a backlog in the drill-press room. This causes two hours of overtime for that department. Two hours' overtime translates to $425.

You will point this out when you give him feedback later so he sees the effect of his actions. This will reinforce why the goals are important and valuable in the first place.

You must be able to draw a direct line between your employees' actions and your organization's success or bottom line. If you can't do this, you probably have no business talking to them about it. For example:

> The district manager of coffee shops wants to discuss with an employee how her newly dyed green hair, multiple facial piercings, and tattoos are not in keeping with the dress code he wants. Personally, he dislikes this look. He says the look is not "professional" and will turn off the clientele. But she works in Greenwich Village in New York City, where this look is very much the norm. His white shirt and tie are more likely to offend the local patrons. He needs to rethink the discussion he planned to have with her.

Even when your employees' performance meets or exceeds goals, identify the impact. Identify how your employees' efforts contributed to your organization's success. When you give positive feedback, include the organization's positive impact to make your feedback that much more powerful. Consider this scenario:

> An employee kept the average wait time at the drive-up window down to three minutes. What is the direct result of his actions? Customers got their food faster. What else? Everyone else in the store hustled quicker to keep up with his pace. What is better or worse now because of what he did? Those customers will tell friends about the speed at this drive-up window. Share one or more of the ways this employee's actions had a positive impact.

Checklist: Measure Results

- ❏ Our measurement tools are efficient. We are not spending more on them than is necessary.
- ❏ Our measurement tools are fair. The data accurately measures what it is supposed to measure.
- ❏ Our measurement tools are simple. In most, if not all cases, they are automated to allow employees to stay focused on their jobs.
- ❏ I record the data collected and I share the data as it becomes available.
- ❏ I appropriately share data to promote healthy competition among my workers.
- ❏ I compare the data collected from my employees' performance with the goals to identify gaps.
- ❏ I identify and understand the impact the data suggests.

CHAPTER 4

✓ Provide Feedback

Feedback is information about behavior and its resulting impact. It may or may not include instruction for improvement as well.

Feedback doesn't solve problems by itself. It opens the door for problem-solving discussions and follow-up actions. Your employees cannot do a good job without feedback, and they certainly can't improve without it.

Honest, direct feedback is a critical component of holding employees accountable. It also helps build a trusting relationship with your employees. They may not agree with what you say, but if you are honest and fair about it, they will learn to trust and respect you. The more they trust and respect you, the greater effect your feedback will have as you hold them accountable for results.

True feedback is a gift. To be effective, you must offer feedback from a place of caring. It must come from a sincere desire on your part to help or support your employees, not merely to "fix" them. If you can't come at it from this perspective, you may fail, no matter what words you choose or methods you use. Intent is more important than technique.

Step 1. Motivate yourself to offer feedback.

The Reasons

There are risks associated with giving feedback. Your employees may not understand the message. They may get hurt, angry, or

defensive. Your relationships with them may even become temporarily strained. It's important to balance those concerns with some
of the benefits you personally gain when you give feedback. While
your employees stand to grow by the information you will share
with them, you will also benefit. Keeping in mind what's in it for
you may be just the motivation you need to move forward when
the idea of giving feedback intimidates or overwhelms you.

The Basics

1. Focus on what you want to accomplish when you give your
   feedback. What is your ultimate objective here? The more
   focused you are, the more successful you will be.
2. Give yourself encouragement by identifying how you will
   also benefit by giving this feedback.

The Details

It's pretty easy to see the benefits your employees will enjoy when
they receive feedback from you. They get valuable information,
they are helped, they get another perspective, and so on. But what's
in it for *you*? Don't worry—you too will personally benefit when
you give good feedback.

- *You clarify expectations.* Any misunderstanding that occurred
  when you set expectations or got commitment from your employees will come out when they start to perform their jobs.
  If you don't say anything, the gap between what you want
  and what your employees think you want just widens. When
  you give feedback, you are able to clarify your expectations
  with real-life situations and relevant examples.
- *You get better employees and better results.* Your feedback will
  improve your employees' performance by calling out what
  needs to be done differently. Better performance from your
  employees will mean better results for you and your organization.
- *You open the door to receive feedback yourself.* If you give
  your employees feedback regularly, they will be encouraged

to give you the feedback you need as well. The more you give feedback, the more you understand how the receiver needs to be open to receive it. Then you will learn to open yourself up to better receive their feedback.

- *You set the example.* When they see you give feedback regularly, your employees will follow your lead. They'll start to offer feedback to others, including their own co-workers. Now your whole team benefits again. And the more you give feedback, the better you'll get at doing it. Soon you'll be coaching your employees on how to give feedback just as well as you do.

- *You get to help someone.* Show that you care. Good feedback is truly a gift. Anyone can criticize, disapprove, or pass judgment. But to give good feedback, you have to care enough to do it well. Your employees know this and will appreciate your effort. You'll then have the satisfaction of knowing that you really helped someone do a better job—perhaps even be a better person.

- *You get to clear the air.* Get whatever bothers you off your chest. Avoid letting the resentment build up. Avoid the bitterness, hostility, and isolation that often come with that resentment. Giving feedback allows you to be forthcoming about how you feel.

- *You strengthen your relationship with your employees.* To give feedback, and to do it well, you have to care enough to be specific. You have to care enough to deliver it in a way that your employees will hear it and accept it. You have to care enough to be honest and straightforward. When you care this much, your intent is much more important than any technique you use. Your message of caring will come across no matter what words you use, and your employees can't help but be affected by your caring. As a result, you will draw closer to each other, your trust in each other will increase, and your relationship will improve.

Step 2. Determine when to deliver your feedback.

The Reasons

Memories fade fast. The sooner you and your employees can discuss what happened, the better all of you will remember it accurately. The better your memories are, the more agreement you'll have on what happened. The more agreement you have, the more likely it is that you'll spend your time and energy on resolutions instead of fighting over the facts of the situation. Time your feedback so that your employees can get the most out of it.

The Basics

1. Offer feedback as soon as possible after you observe the behavior or action.
2. Time the feedback so that your employees are ready and able to hear the message.
3. Avoid giving constructive feedback when others are present.
4. It may be appropriate to give positive feedback in front of others, but that depends on how comfortable your employees are with public recognition and attention.
5. Avoid giving feedback when your employees are tired, busy, upset, or otherwise distracted or unable to hear it.

The Details

The more serious the feedback, the sooner you should give it. No one wants to hear weeks or months later that she is doing something wrong or performing poorly. Similarly, positive feedback will have less of a reinforcing effect if it is delivered long after the action happened.

Don't be so overly zealous, though, that you give feedback before your employees are ready to hear it. Consider this example:

> Your employee gives a presentation to one of your clients. The employee sits next to you when he is finished and whispers,

"How'd I do?" Now is not the time to give detailed feedback, even if you have much to say. Perhaps offer a quick, "Just fine." Then wait until the meeting is over and the employee is in a better frame of mind to really focus on what you have to say. But don't wait too long, either. Weeks later, much of the effect of your detailed feedback on that presentation will be lost.

Step 3. Set the stage for a positive interaction.

The Reasons

For feedback to be effective, your employees have to believe that what you say is real and valid. They need to believe that you are giving feedback to be helpful, not using it as a hammer to beat them. Creating the right environment will make it easier for them to hear and receive your feedback in the spirit you intend.

The Basics

1. Choose a location that is private, quiet, and free of distractions.
2. Let your employee know that you want to provide some feedback.
3. Express your positive intent.

The Details

When you're ready to let your employee know how you feel about her performance, it can be as simple as telling her that you want to discuss the issue. Depending on your relationship, it may be more appropriate just to ask if you can give her feedback now. For example:

- "Can I give you some feedback on that?"
- "I'd like to talk about what just happened here."
- "Can you meet with me this afternoon at two o-clock? I'm concerned about how the project is going and I want to discuss it with you."

Employees need to know right away that you are not out to "get" them. They need to know that you have a positive reason for giving them feedback—positive for you *and* them. You don't want to come across as trying to attack or place blame. When they believe your intentions are positive, they are more likely to listen to and act on your feedback.

Pointing to a common goal may help express your positive intent. For example:

- "We need to be sure that every customer wants to come back and do business with us again. I'd like to discuss . . ."
- "Can we talk about our new closing procedures? I'm concerned that these changes aren't helping us meet our goal to be out of here by midnight."

Make sure your employees are ready to hear the message. You want them to accept your comments in the spirit you give them. Even if you think the timing is right and that you've set the stage for a productive conversation, your employees may still not be ready. Outside influences may interfere, like a fight at lunch with a friend or concern for a sick relative. Watch your employee's body language, tone of voice, eye contact, and other clues that will signal whether he is ready to hear your feedback.

This is true even when you want to give positive feedback. You know this person. Use your understanding to gauge when conditions are good for a fruitful discussion before you proceed. He may not be ready for positive feedback when he's fixating on something that did not go well, or if he is embarrassed hearing the praise. Occasionally, it may be better to postpone even a positive discussion rather than have it when someone's not ready for it.

Step 4. Be specific about what you observed.

The Reasons

Constructive feedback is more likely to be heard if it is based on facts, not judgment or inferences. Agree to the facts of what hap-

pened first. Then together you can interpret those facts and ultimately find resolution. Your employees won't be ready to change
anything until they understand and accept what they did and why
their actions matter to you and your organization.

Positive feedback is no different. Your employees will not truly
grasp what actions you want them to repeat until they understand
and accept specifically what they did and how their choices affect
the company as a whole.

The Basics

1. Comment on what happened factually. You should be able
   to precede your comments with phrases like "I saw," "I no-
   ticed," "I observed," "I heard," and so on.
2. Use facts and figures whenever possible.
3. Leave interpretation and innuendo out of it. Stick to what
   happened without judgment, comment, or analysis.

The Details

Here's how to give feedback based on facts, not judgments.

Spell out the action. Don't label it. Here's where the gap analysis
you did in step 6 of Chapter 3 pays off. For example:

> Your employee was late for work twice in one week. Say, "I
> noticed you were more than ten minutes late for work two days
> last week." It's factual. She either was or was not late. There
> should be little discussion. Once your employee agrees to these
> facts, you can move on to the next step.
>
> You could have said, "You're frequently tardy," or even,
> "You were frequently tardy last week." Either of these state-
> ments encourages your employee to be offended by the label
> tardy. Moreover, you invite an argument of semantics by using
> the word *frequently*. Is twice in one week frequent, just occa-
> sional, or even sporadic? Your employee will immediately take
> a defensive position, not a good place to start a productive con-
> versation.

Do not suggest how to improve. Comments should be made in the past tense because you are only talking about what happened and not what *should* happen (yet!). If you find yourself using words like *should, could, ought, need, suggesting, must,* or similar words that hint at a fix, back off for now. For instance:

> Your employee was late for work twice in one week. Say, "I noticed you were more than ten minutes late for work two days last week." Do not yet cloud the facts by talking about what you want, such as, "You need to be on time more often!" Although this may be what you ultimately require, your employee first needs to understand where this demand is coming from. He will either ask why you are saying this now or claim he is on time already. Either way, he needs the specific facts that are driving your demand now. That will put you back to being specific about past behavior. So just start there. Don't make your employee have to get you there with a defensive remark.

Avoid vague comments. General comments are easier to make than specific ones. But they are not as helpful at pinpointing exact behaviors or actions that need to be addressed. Your employee may be left wondering what you meant, or be misguided altogether.

> It's easier to say, "Your presentation wasn't very organized" than to specify what facts made you think it wasn't organized enough (specific feedback).

Even with positive feedback, vague comments don't pinpoint the exact behaviors or actions that you want repeated. Your employee may end up not continuing the behavior that you thought you were reinforcing.

> Saying, "Your presentation was well organized" is easy, but it isn't specific about what about the presentation was so well organized.

General comments also may *feel* safer to make. You're not really saying anything that can be refuted, right? Wrong. Managers who favor vague feedback mistakenly believe this is a good way to avoid conflict with their employees. But vague comments masquerading as feedback are rarely safe. Your employee will usually have one of two responses. She may discount the feedback as not really having merit, and nothing happens. Or worse, she will object to the vague generality, not understand it, and challenge the manager. Conflict, the very thing the manager hoped to avoid, is now inevitable. Consider this scenario:

> *Manager:* "You need to be friendlier to the customers,"
> *Employee (challenges):* "What? What do you mean, friendlier?"
> *Manager:* "Hey, I'm not trying to start an argument here. You were just a little curt with that last one and so I was politely asking you to be friendlier, that's all."
> *Employee:* "First, you did not ask, you ordered. Second, I don't know how you can possibly accuse me of being curt. I mean, did you see what she did when I first approached her? She . . ."
>
> And the conflict is full-blown. A better approach would be to avoid the vague comments and start off with a specific observation of fact: "I just heard you call that customer a jerk. Then you slammed the register shut and told her that . . ."

Avoid absolute statements. Avoid using words like *always* and *never*. Rarely are such statements completely true. When you make generalizations, you invite an argument, or at the least a defensive reaction. Be accurate and specific and avoid the clash. For example:

> You might say, "You are always late coming back from your break." Your employee will predictably be able to cite examples of when he was not late coming back from break. When he does, you lose credibility for making a blanket statement that was not completely true.

Keep it brief. Granted, being specific takes more words than a label or a vague reference. Just don't start to ramble. Make your point, give your feedback, and stop. There is no need to defend what you

said, overexplain it, or even try to sell it. Here are some examples
of solid, brief feedback:

- "This display case is not set up according to the vendor's
  spec."
- "You rolled your eyes three times just now while Karen was
  speaking."
- "There are two used napkins on the counter."

Be just as rigorous with positive feedback. Reinforce great behavior
with feedback that is specific and focused. The more specific your
comments, the more your employees are able to continue the valuable work they do. See the difference here:

> Your employee gives a safety presentation in a staff meeting.
> A comment like "good job" may feel good to your employee
> momentarily, but she won't know exactly what about her work
> is particularly valued. For the next presentation, will she focus
> more on the funny jokes that lightened up the group? Or will she
> focus on not looking at her notes?
>
> Specific positive feedback eliminates the guesswork. "I like
> the way you were able to link our common practices to the
> OSHA guidelines and make them come alive for everyone."
> Now your employee knows what about the presentation was so
> good. Next time she will link current practices to guidelines and
> create relevancy.

The feeling of goodwill stays much longer with employees when
you are specific about your positive feedback. Days, weeks, or even
months from now your employees will still remember the specific
feedback you gave today. It will encourage them for some time.

Tailor your feedback to your audience. Some employees prefer
softer words. Some employees prefer intense eye contact. Some employees prefer greater physical distance from you when you talk to
them. You know your employees. Individualize the way you give
feedback to employees based on what you know about them. Cater

to each person's needs and preferences. Remember, this is not about making you feel comfortable. It's about helping your employees receive the information they need to be the best they can be.

Step 5. Focus on the behavior or action, not the person or attitude.

The Reasons

Stay focused on the behaviors and you'll avoid endless arguments about attitude, intention, and other intangibles that you can never know for sure. Remember, while attitude may drive behavior, ultimately you are really only paying for behavior.

The Basics

1. Do not mention attitude, intention, or any other intangible attribute.
2. Start by thinking about your employee's bad attitude (or intention, etc.).
3. Ask yourself, "How do I know he has a bad attitude? What behaviors have I seen or heard (or not) that demonstrate a bad attitude?"
4. Keep asking those questions; push yourself to answer them in more and more detail.
5. When you have pinpointed behaviors that you can literally see, hear, or feel, you have translated the "attitude" into concrete actions. Focus your feedback on these.

The Details

Remember, you will need to narrow down what you call "attitude" to concrete, observable actions. For example:

> Your employee has a bad attitude. You just know it. But how do you know that he has a bad attitude? Well, he comes back from his lunch break late more often than not—even when he knows

the counter is busy. How else do you know? He is lazy. This is still a label, so what does he do that demonstrates this to you? Well, whenever there is a break in customer flow, he doesn't do anything but stand there and wait for the next customer. Now, you could give this feedback: "You have a bad attitude and are lazy." While this may ease your burden, it will hardly be productive. If you say it that way, plan on a defensive reaction or a counterattack.

A better approach would be: "I saw that you were late coming back from lunch three times in a row this week. Also, when there is a break in customer flow, you stand there and do nothing." This is more behavior-based. There will be less discussion about whether these facts are true. You can move on quickly to the next step and to resolution.

You cannot see an attitude. All you can see are behaviors and actions. Attitude is entirely inside your employee. Only she can verify what her attitude is. You only see behaviors that may indicate one attitude or another—but they do not confirm it. So why go there? Compare this scenario to the one outlined above:

Your employee is cheerful and pleasant as she changes her patients' bedpans. If appropriate, she makes polite conversation while doing this task. But she hates to change bedpans. She thinks it is a task that should belong to another job classification. She has never shared this with anyone and doesn't plan to. So on the inside, her attitude might be considered bad, but on the outside, you and the patient see something very different. Her behaviors and actions are exactly what is required. Does it really matter what her attitude is when her performance is so good?

Avoid labels. Adhere to this rule even when the label feels so obviously true: Rude is rude. Uncooperative is uncooperative. Not being a team player is not being a team player. Plain and simple, right? Maybe, but there are still concrete behaviors that indicate these things to you. Whenever one word or phrase constitutes your feedback, you are probably labeling or overgeneralizing. Single-word feedback is not specific enough to really help your employee, even if it's positive, as in the following example.

> Your employee writes a report. If you say, "Good job," what will your employee continue to do with future reports? Use the same font? Use the same bullet format? Forgo an executive summary again? Turn it in one day late again to heighten the interest? For the same report, if you say, "Too long," how will your employee shorten it for you next time? Use a small type font? Cut the historical data? Use more abbreviations?

Stay away from labels by asking yourself the same questions as for attitude. "How do I know my employee is Label X? What is he doing that shows me his Label X-ness? What have I seen or heard (or not) that proves he is Label X?" Let's look at an illustration of this idea.

> Your employee is obviously annoyed with a coworker and is blowing her off. You could say, "You just blew her off." This is not very precise. How do you know he blew her off? He rolled his eyes three times while she was talking. He made little eye contact as he mostly looked out the window. He shook his head repeatedly as she explained her point.
>
> Point out these behaviors rather than interpreting them as blowing her off. "I observed that you rolled your eyes three times. You looked out the window as she spoke rather than making eye contact. And you shook your head repeatedly as she made her points." Either this did or did not happen. Your conversation can continue as soon as he acknowledges that these things occurred.

Even if your employee does have a "bad attitude" or is "obviously not very committed to the job," what can you do about it? Find the behavior in front of that attitude and address it. Addressing the attitude is a no-win proposition, as in:

Manager: "I don't like your attitude toward the customers who complain."

Employee: "Oh? And what attitude is that?"

Manager: "Well, you just seem dismissive, and we want you to have a good attitude toward all our customers, not just the happy ones."

Employee: "How do you know that I don't have a good attitude with them? For your information, I do! The problem is not my attitude, it's our crummy product."

Manager: "Oh, so now you have an attitude about what we produce?"

And on the conversation goes, in a downward spiral.

Step 6. Never use the word *but*.

The Reasons

It negates everything that came before it. Most people translate the word *but* to mean, "Please disregard everything you've heard up to this point because you are about to hear the honest truth." Although when giving positive feedback followed by constructive feedback it is typical to bridge the two with *but*, don't.

The Basics

Replace the *but* with the word *and*. It is always grammatically correct and doesn't negate the positive feedback like *but* does. For instance:

Your employee prepares a report for you. You can say, "Great job on the report. I love the three columns that make it easy to compare the data from the three states, **but** I think forcing all the data on one page makes it difficult to read through it." The first part of the feedback, very positive, is negated by the second part and its *but*.

Change one word and you get: "Great job on the report. I love the three columns that make it easy to compare the data from the three states, and I think forcing all the data on one page made it difficult to read through it." Now both parts feel equally represented and valued.

The Details

Remember these ways that the word *but* can cause problems.

But *often precedes a fix.* At this point, you just want to comment on what you observed. You're not ready to resolve anything until your employees accept the feedback on the facts. Once they do, they are ready to work on making changes. So don't throw out a fix too early. Focus the feedback on what happened first. See what happens in this example:

> "Great job on the report. I love the three columns that make it easy to compare the data from the three states, but next time . . ." Now we're headed into a fix. Just stop after the positive feedback. Let it sink in.
>
> If there is an area for improvement, add it after an *and*: "Great job on the report. I love the three columns that make it easy to compare the data from the three states, and I didn't like that it was forced onto one page with such a small font size." No fix yet, just information about what was.

Avoid the **but** *even if it precedes a positive comment. But* discounts whatever precedes it. You may consider switching the common order by putting a constructive comment first, then a *but*, then a positive comment. This may be tempting for managers who shy away from confrontation, since the constructive comment is downplayed. The risk is that your employee may not really hear the constructive part of the feedback, as in this example:

> "You need to count the change back to the customer in every transaction, but you seem to be doing a great job balancing your drawer every night without a variance of more than twenty-five cents." Your employee may hear this to mean that counting

change back to the customer isn't all that important because he is so good at balancing all the time.

Balance the two pieces with *and*: "You need to count the change back to the customer in every transaction, and you seem to be doing a great job balancing your drawer every night without a variance of more than twenty-five cents."

Beware the but *lookalikes.* There are several words that mean the same thing as *but* or are used for the same purpose. Avoid using words like *however, yet, although, still, except, nevertheless, nonetheless, though,* and any other word or phrase that suggests what precedes it is not as important as what follows it.

Step 7. Explain the impact on the organization.

The Reasons

You don't give feedback just to give feedback. There has to be a reason. Feedback around the specifics of your employee's behavior is the *what* of your conversation. Feedback about the impact that behavior had on your organization is the *why* of it. The impact helps you both stay objective as you focus together on the overall success of your organization.

The Basics

1. Try to quantify the organizational impact of individual behaviors so it is less subjective. Objective information is easier to accept.
2. Relate your employee's action to its impact on the organization.

The Details

Be specific. What are the objective, observable effects of your employees' actions? They may have affected customer satisfaction, employee morale, cost, time, amount of rework, and so on. (Here is where your work in step 7 of Chapter 3 really pays off.) For instance:

> Your employee was late for work twice last week. You say, "You were more than ten minutes late for work two days last week. This caused Logan to have to work your station and get behind on his own workload by four units each time."

Not all impact is readily quantifiable. You may have to approximate or even guess at what the impact was if it's not immediately clear or is intangible.

> Your employee interrupted a co-worker several times in a meeting. She also made disparaging remarks about this co-worker's point of view. After giving the feedback in factual, specific terms, you then explain the impact: "I'm concerned that your co-worker felt devalued in the meeting. Her face looked sad. She stopped contributing altogether, and we lost the value of her insight and perspective. I also fear others saw the way you treated her, and they began to hold back. We lost their insights as well."

Don't blame. List only one or two of the most important impacts of your employees' behavior. They need to hear the impact, but listing more than a couple may be misinterpreted as your trying to fix blame. You just need to say enough to get across the seriousness of the behavior, and to motivate a desire to problem-solve, no more.

Back up positive feedback. Specific, focused, positive feedback is good. Make it really powerful by connecting the behavior you're recognizing with its positive impact on the organization. Then your employees will understand what they did well and why it's so important that they did it, as in the following illustration:

> Your employee handled a disgruntled customer well. You say, "Good job with that customer. I especially liked the way you kept your voice calm and steady, even when hers got high and

screechy. She even cussed at you once, and you responded calmly, without swearing." This is specific feedback on what your employee did.

Now add the impact. "Your calm response led that customer to calm down herself. She even apologized to me later for her outburst. You saved us from losing a customer and the bad word-of-mouth advertising that would have accompanied that." Stated this way, your feedback becomes much more relevant and powerful.

Step 8. Understand your employees' perspective.

The Reasons

You can't take meaningful action to resolve issues together until you understand each other. After you give your feedback, your employees may understand you, but you don't necessarily understand them yet. Now is the time to open the door for two-way communication.

The Basics

1. Invite your employees to share their responses.
2. Be open not only to what is said but also to how it is said. Listen to tone of voice; watch body language.
3. Clarify any misunderstandings.
4. Summarize what you heard before moving on.

The Details

Invite the employee's response. Often you don't even have to ask. Simply give your feedback and explain the impact. Then stop talking. Look the employee in the eye and just wait for her to say something. Usually, she will engage right then and there.

If your employee doesn't offer a response, gently ask for one. Avoid closed-ended questions that will only give you a yes or no. Use open-ended questions to encourage conversation. For example:

- "What do you think?"
- "How do you see it?"
- "Please tell me what your thoughts are."
- "What's your take on this?"

Be genuinely curious about an employee's perspective. Don't assume you know his answer, or even his position on the issue. You may be surprised to learn something that completely changes how you regard the situation. Be open to the idea that you may have been wrong about something, have inaccurate data, or may have jumped to a conclusion unfairly or prematurely.

Listen objectively. You will get a sense of the employee's emotional reaction. Hurt? Surprised? Angry? Scared? Eager to hear more? Closed down? All are legitimate reactions. Each requires you to handle things differently to keep the meeting productive. Watch and listen for signals that will tell you what your employee is feeling and where she may need your help to move forward.

How your employee responds will also give you cues for where to take the conversation next, how fast to go, and even how far. He may or may not even be ready to continue the discussion at all right now. If so, it's entirely appropriate to disengage briefly. Let your employee gather himself. Come back together when he is prepared to have a productive, problem-solving discussion. Take a look at this situation:

> You give feedback to your employee, who responds strongly. You feel it's best to postpone the discussion. "I can see this really upsets you, Lynn. I don't want to go further until you are ready. How about if we talk about this again tomorrow morning when you get in?" You don't have to say more than that. Overnight, your employee can process her reaction. She should be ready to move forward tomorrow.

On the other hand, your employee may be very aware of the issue and even anxious to find resolutions that will work. Don't let him rush the speed at which you address issues, but certainly consider his capability, interest level, and commitment as you move the dialogue forward.

Your employees' reactions may be feedback to you. Employees will give you feedback on how you delivered your feedback to them. They may not say a word, but their body language and other reactions will give you clues about how effective you are. The more objectively your employees respond to your feedback, the more likely it is that you are delivering it objectively. You may be surprised, too, when your employees actually thank you for caring enough to give them feedback. When feedback is a true gift, the receiver accepts and appreciates it as such.

Summarize. Make sure you understand what you heard. Summarizing proves to your employee that you were really listening. Summarizing your employee's response doesn't necessarily mean that you agree. It just shows that you heard her point of view, understand it, and respect it:

> "So what I heard you say, Caroline, is that you don't think it's fair that I single you out when others made inappropriate comments to the vendor. You think that I should be talking to JT, Steve, and Aaron as well, right?" By saying this, you have not agreed to anything. Nor have you committed to talking to anyone else. You are just checking to make sure you understand Caroline's perspective.

Summarizing often helps reduce negative tension if things have started to go awry. If you listen to your employee, she is much more apt to listen to you. The lines of communication remain open. Your discussion remains productive.

Step 9. Offer a suggestion, if appropriate.

The Reasons

Most employees will know what to do after they get your feedback. Most do not need you to spell out how their behavior should change. For those who do need help, now is the time—*after* you have given the feedback and *after* you have heard their response to it. Offer a suggestion. Yes, as the manager you could make it an edict, mandate, or order. But you are more likely to get a positive response if you "suggest." The rules for giving a suggestion are similar to those for giving feedback.

The Basics

1. Don't precede the suggestion with the word *but* or you will discount everything that came before it.
2. Choose your words carefully. There is a big difference in how strongly you come across based on the words you use.
3. Be specific. Don't leave your employees wondering what exactly you want them to do to improve.
4. Focus on the behavior or action you want to see, not the person or an attitude.
5. Explain the impact that following your suggestion will have on your organization, your employee, or both.

The Details

Never use the word **but**. It bears repeating here. *But* is most often used to connect a positive tidbit of feedback to a detailed description of what should be fixed and how, where, and when that should be done. If you are going to combine feedback with a suggestion, bridge it with the word *and*. Look at the difference below:

> "Great job with that customer. I really liked the way you listened intently as he complained about his sandwich. You didn't interrupt him or disagree with his perspective at all. You nodded empathetically. All those things told him that you cared and were interested. That's what we want all of our customers to feel, *but* next time don't blame Heidee for the mix-up in front of the customer. Just tell the customer that . . ." Your comments that

preceded the *but* are negated by it. You want your employee to hear that positive reinforcement and continue to respond to customer complaints as he did. You also need him to understand how he could have handled the situation even better.

Try again, replacing the *but* with an *and*. "Great job with that customer. I really liked the way you listened intently as he complained about his sandwich. You didn't interrupt him or disagree with his perspective at all. You nodded empathetically. All those things told him that you cared and were interested. That's what we want all of our customers to feel, *and* next time don't blame Heidee for the mix-up in front of the customer. Just tell the customer that . . ." The whole tone of the suggestion changes, and your employee will be more willing to accept both pieces of what you have to say.

Be deliberate in your choice of words. The words you use indicate how directive your suggestion will be. A very directive approach includes phrases like *you must, you have to, you need to,* and *you had better.* The suggestion becomes more like an order. At the other end of the spectrum are phrases like *would you, could you, you may want to, perhaps consider,* and *what about trying this.* The suggestion becomes more of a request. Neither is good nor bad. You just need to decide how strongly you want to come across in each situation and with each employee. Your relationship with your employee and how strongly you feel about something will drive how directive you choose to be. Take a look at this example:

"Next time, you had better prop his head up like this before the subsequent procedure" is very directive. If propping the head is a safety or health issue, this strong approach may be necessary. If it is a matter of your own convenience or makes the next procedure easier, you could say, "Next time, you may want to prop his head up like this before the subsequent procedure." The words are less directive and indicate more individual discretion is allowed.

Be specific with your direction. Avoid vague hints and clues. Don't be afraid to ask directly for what you want or need. This is not being pushy, overbearing, or demanding. This is you doing your job as a manager and helping your employees see what the organization needs from them. Here's another example:

> It's easier to say, "You need to be more prepared next time you make a presentation to the staff." It's general and doesn't require you to put much thought into what you really want. Unfortunately, it also doesn't tell your employee what to change. Should she have her note cards typed up? Should she have better visual aids? Should she have the presentation completely memorized? Left with only hints, your employee would be justified in doing any one of those things and believe that she is improving as you directed.
>
> It is much better to be more specific and say, "Using note cards is fine as long as you give a lot of eye contact to your audience. Also, you need to make sure that your PowerPoint slides are in the same order as the handout." Now you have defined what prepared means to you and left your employee with no question about what is expected next time.

Focus on the behavior or action, not the person or attitude. You cannot measure an attitude change. You can measure a change in behavior that may indicate an improved attitude. Focus on the behaviors and the attitude will take care of itself.

If you want to suggest your employee get a better attitude or be more committed to the job or show better teamwork (a label), what can you do? Start by thinking about what you want from him. Then ask yourself, "How will I know when his X is better? What will I see or hear (or not) when he is exhibiting better X? What will he actually do differently when he is more X?" Your answers will be the behaviors your employee needs to change for improvement, as shown below:

You want to tell your employee to show more teamwork. "Show more teamwork" is vague and open to much interpretation, since "teamwork" is just a label. So ask yourself the questions:

"How will I know it when he shows more teamwork?"
He will think through the impact his actions and decisions will have on the team before making them.

"What will I see when he is exhibiting teamwork?"
He will ask his team members for input on the decisions he makes before making them.

As the manager, you need to point out these desirable behaviors rather than make your employee try to guess them from "Show more teamwork." Say instead, "When making decisions, add a step: Consider the impact of this decision on your team members. When you see that it could affect your teammates, involve them in the decision-making process—ask their perspective, get their input, or give them a heads up." You can then measure whether these things happen or not. You won't find yourself having an argument later when your employee brings in doughnuts twice in one week to demonstrate his teamwork.

Tailor your feedback to your audience. Different employees respond differently to the way you communicate. Individualize the way you give a suggestion for each employee based on what you know of that person. Cater to her needs or preferences. Remember, this is not about making you feel superior, strong, or in control. It's about helping your employee learn a way to be more successful at work. Put your feedback in a way that she can hear it, accept it, and use it.

Explain why you made the suggestion. You give a suggestion because you believe that if your employee follows it, the organization will benefit, right? Your employee should know what the expected benefit or impact will be. It will help both of you to remain objective about the suggestion as you focus on what's best for your organization. Consider this scenario:

> "I need you to change the way you did this report. You need to put this data in a table with the three regions across the top and the cost items on the left." Your employee certainly can do what you requested here, but you'll get better commitment if you add, "This will make it easier to compare the results of the three regions. It will be more likely that people will look at more of the data. Also, it will help the board members review the information quicker so that they can be more efficient in their meeting."
>
> With solid reasons for doing what is requested, your employee is more likely not just to comply but to commit to excellence.

Suggestions will limit your employee's choices. Give feedback. If you immediately offer a suggestion about how to improve, your employee now has only two options: Do what you just prescribed, or don't change at all. Let's see what that looks like:

> The feedback: "You got three customer complaints this week. They all said you sounded insincere and cold. They felt you didn't care about them as people; you just wanted to get the claim paid quickly."
>
> The suggestion: "From now on, I want you to make sure you use the customer's name at least twice on each call. I want you to make at least one empathetic statement that will convince them you care."
>
> This suggestion is very descriptive and directive. While it may be appropriate for a new employee, an experienced employee might find it offensive. He will either follow the new guidelines or continue to fall short of expectations.

For most employees, suggestions are not necessary. Merely give them your feedback about what occurred and its impact. Stop. They will most likely identify several options available and then figure out which will work best for them in this situation. Don't be

surprised, though, if your employees ask for your input, as shown
in the next example:

> "You got three customer complaints this week. They all said you
> sounded insincere and cold. They felt you didn't care about
> them as people; you just wanted to get the claim paid quickly."
>
> Stop. Ask, "How do you think you can turn this perception
> around?"
>
> You just might hear something like: "Well, I guess if I used
> their name more often, that could make it seem more personal.
> I could also put up this smiley face in front of me to remind me
> to smile. I know others can feel a smile over the phone. I also
> might . . ."
>
> Your employee's ideas here are more likely to bring about
> the true sincerity you and your customers are looking for.

Checklist: Provide Feedback

- ❏ I understand not only how my employees will gain from receiving my feedback, but also how I will benefit by giving it.
- ❏ I give feedback as soon as possible after I observe the behavior
  or action, making sure my employees are ready to hear it.
- ❏ I always give constructive feedback in private. I may give positive feedback in public when I'm confident that my employees would appreciate that.
- ❏ I set the stage for a positive interaction before jumping into
  giving feedback.
- ❏ I describe specifically what I observed, sticking to what actually transpired without adding judgment, comment, or analysis.
- ❏ I avoid making generalizations and using words like *always*
  and *never.*
- ❏ I avoid talking about attitudes, intentions, or labels in place
  of behaviors and actions.
- ❏ I avoid using the word *but.*

❏ I explain objectively the impact my employees' behavior had on the organization.

❏ I seek to understand my employees' perspective of the situation.

❏ I offer a suggestion for how to improve only if my employees truly need one or ask for one.

CHAPTER 5

✓ Link to Consequences

You have set goals that are specific, measureable, action-oriented, realistic, and time-bound. Your employee has committed to reaching them. You have measured the results. You have given feedback. In most cases, this process will ensure great employee performance. Setting expectations followed by quality feedback is the backbone of holding someone accountable.

Sometimes, however, your employees will need a little more help to live up to their commitments. When they struggle to reach their goals, you can help by administering appropriate consequences. Consequences will guide and focus their behavior and encourage them to take their commitments more seriously.

Step 1. Determine what consequence(s) should apply.

The Reasons

Your purpose in using consequences is not to punish your employee but to help him or her get back on track, performing well again.

Punishment and consequences are not the same thing. Consequences are what your employees will experience as a natural result of their behavior. Consequences will help them to refocus and recommit. Punishment includes those things added on to make your employees "pay" for their mistakes. Punishments do not contribute to helping your employees improve their behavior. They often foster resentment, hurt, or a desire to rebel. For instance:

> Your employee has not been wearing his seat belt when driving company vehicles. An appropriate consequence would be to reassign him to work that doesn't require driving. This way, your employee is no longer as much of a danger to himself. A punishment would be to deny his vacation request because he didn't wear his seat belt, when otherwise you would have granted it.

Leave the "punishment fits the crime" approach to the criminal justice system. You are not dealing with criminals. You are working with decent adults who deserve to be treated with dignity and respect. Focus on what's important here—helping your employees meet their goals. Take action or administer consequences that will move them in that direction. Don't worry about whether you've made your employees pay for any errors, infractions, or slip-ups. Any action you take in response to your employees' behavior should be productive and aimed at helping them improve their performance.

The Basics

1. Check with your boss or human resources department before taking any formal disciplinary action.
2. Consider what consequence makes the most sense for your employee in a given situation.
3. Anticipate how your employee will respond to the action you take and plan accordingly.

The Details

Your choices may be limited. HR policies, union agreements, company rules, precedents, bylaws, and other standards may dictate what form your consequences take. Check before taking action on your own. Modify the following steps to accommodate any parameters already in place.

Choose sensible consequences. They should be aimed at moving your employees to greater performance. That is the only valid purpose for a consequence.

Consequences should also fit how serious the situation is. For example:

> Coming to work late once last month is not as serious as the cash drawer being out of balance a third time this week, which is also not as serious as sexually harassing a co-worker today. Different consequences would apply in these cases.

Consider how similar situations have been handled in the past— not only how you have addressed them but also how other managers in your organization have handled similar situations. Consider any extenuating circumstances that make this situation different from those in the past.

It may be helpful to ask human resources, a colleague, or a trusted associate to give you another perspective. (Never consult with your employee's peers or teammates, though.) An outsider's unbiased view will help you stay fair and objective. Choose someone who will keep the situation you share confidential.

Anticipate how your employee may react. Will she be hurt? Surprised? Quiet? Defensive? Whatever the answer, plan your approach accordingly. Have tissues on hand. Have a witness present—shop steward, human resources rep, another manager. Bring notes to help you remember what you want to say. Do whatever you need to do to be prepared for how you expect your employee to react. Again, a trusted confidant can help you plan properly.

Step 2. Remind your employee of his prior commitment.

The Reasons

Here is the value of gaining your employee's commitment or buy-in back when you did. You can hold him accountable for not living up to that commitment. Had he merely "accepted" the goals without "committing" to them, you'd be in a position of selling the goals and their importance now.

You already gave your employee feedback on her actual performance and its impact on the organization. Make sure that she sees how her results fell short of what she committed to achieve.

The Basics

1. Remind your employee of the commitment he made to the goal(s).
2. Ask your employee for her comments, perspective, or view of the situation.

The Details

Review your employee's commitment to reaching his goals. Remind him of the goal(s), if necessary. Remind him of the commitment he made to reach the goal. This is especially important if this is not the first time you're dealing with this employee on this issue.

Let your employee speak. Let her tell you more about how she sees the situation. Use open-ended questions that invite conversation:

- "What can you tell me about this?"
- "Is there something I should know about this?"
- "What's your take on this?"

Stay away from questions that sound more like what a parent would say to a child, and thus put your employee on the defensive:

- "So, what do you have to say for yourself?"
- "(Sigh) What's your side of the story?"
- "Why do we have to deal with this (again)?"

Listen attentively to your employee's response. Regardless of how he responds, your objective is to maintain his dignity and self-esteem. Show empathy, even if you feel like you've heard his excuses before. You can show empathy and still be firm in delivering consequences.

The main thing to watch for is an indication that the action or consequence you have planned is, in fact, an appropriate one. The only way you can do this, however, is to be truly open to what your employee has to say. Be open to the possibility that there may be information that she has that you do not. That information may change what you have planned.

Be sure you understand what your employee has said by summarizing it back to him. Check your understanding before moving on:

> "Okay, let me make sure I have this straight. You helped out quite a bit in Purchasing when Ruth went on maternity leave. And you feel that since that took so much of your time, you shouldn't be held to this goal anymore, at least not to the original deadline. Is that correct?"

Step 3. Spell out what action you will take and why.

The Reasons

You may take formal action or informal action at this point. Many organizations refer to formal action as disciplinary action, positive discipline, corrective action, being put on notice, or being written up. Avoid thinking of discipline as a form of punishment. The two are not necessarily the same. As long as you stick with the definition of discipline as "training that develops self-control or character," you'll be fine.

The Basics

1. At most organizations, formal action requires that you follow specific guidelines and documentation. Adjust the following to satisfy those conditions. Check with your boss or human resources department before taking formal disciplinary action.
2. Be specific and clear about what the action is and what it means.

3. Explain why you are taking this action.

4. Warn your employee of future action that may be required if the problem is not resolved.

The Details

Don't beat around the bush. If you are taking formal action—disciplinary, corrective, or otherwise—call it out. Be clear about what is happening and why. For example:

> "This is a formal oral warning and will be documented as such. It is the first step in our Progressive Discipline Program. The seriousness of driving a company vehicle without wearing your seat belt warrants this formal action."

If this is not the first time you are having this discussion with this employee, remind her of prior discussions and what consequences were promised then, as in:

> "The last time you drove a company vehicle without a seat belt, I warned you that another occurrence would require that I take corrective action. This constitutes a formal oral warning and will be documented as such. It is the first step in our Progressive Discipline Program. The seriousness of driving a company vehicle without wearing your seat belt warrants this formal action."

Tempting as it may be, now is not the time to gloat or scold with an "I told you so" comment. There is no need for smugness. Such an approach will not help you maintain your employee's self-esteem or dignity. In fact, it may even make him more defiant. So don't say this:

> "The last time you drove a company vehicle without a seat belt, I warned you that another occurrence would require that I take corrective action. Didn't I tell you that? And now here we are. Somehow I knew this would happen. This constitutes a formal oral warning and will be documented as such. Maybe this time you'll take our seat belt policy seriously."

The less commentary you add, the better. Stay short, focused, and to the point.

Spell out the specifics of the action. Your employee must fully understand what is happening. If you are taking formal action, tell him what that means. Your employee will have many questions he may not even ask. Who else will know about this? How and where will this be documented? Does this affect my eligibility rights to bid for jobs outside of this department? Will this affect my performance review or my raise? How long will this be active? Anticipate such questions like this:

> "This write-up will be documented and placed in your personnel file. After one year, it will be destroyed. Tomorrow I will give you the only other copy I will make. During this one-year period, you may bid for jobs within this department but not for jobs in other departments. This write-up alone will not affect your performance review or your raises. Do you have any questions about what this write-up means to you and your status here?"

Also, tell your employee if the way she works will be changed at all. Will you be monitoring her more closely? Will you be double-checking her work? Will she have to seek your approval for certain transactions? For instance, you might say:

> "Since these kinds of errors affect so many customers, Gail will be spot-checking your work for the next three weeks to be sure that you have the problem corrected. After that time period, we'll reassess the situation and determine if her audits are still needed."

Answer any and all the questions your employee has. You know this employee. Anticipate what you think he will want to know and just tell him. Don't wait to be asked. Volunteer information. The better your employee understands the consequence, the more effective that consequence will be in helping him to improve.

Tell your employee why you are doing this. You are taking this action to help her improve her performance. That is the objective. Oral warnings, coaching sessions, written reminders, and even probationary periods and suspensions are all designed to remind employees of their commitment to do their jobs well. Use these tools to remind employees of how serious it is when the job doesn't get done well.

You are also being fair to your other employees. You owe it to them to be fair and consistent in the way that you administer such action. They have a right to expect this employee to fulfill his share of the team's responsibilities. You are reminding him of this obligation too.

Explain the future action you may take if necessary. Your employee needs to know what further action you may be required to take if she does not resolve her performance problem. If formal action is a possibility, say so now. This is not a threat. It is a fair warning. Your employee should know what the likely consequences will be to her personally if she continues to behave as she has been. Such a warning might look like this:

> "This is a formal oral warning and will be documented as such. The seriousness of driving a company vehicle without wearing your seat belt warrants this formal action. If you continue to drive without a seat belt, you will subject yourself to further corrective action up to and including possible termination."

Step 4. Own the action you are taking.

The Reasons

Your employee needs to see you as strong and in control here. If not, he may try to make you feel like it's your fault that he's in this predicament. He may try to get you to back down. He may try to shift the responsibility and ownership of the problem to you. What you own is the responsibility to help him resolve the problem quickly and effectively.

Don't let your employee make you out to be the bad guy. You can still be compassionate, caring, and sensitive even when you are firm in administering disciplinary or other action.

The Basics

1. Explain the action you are taking without using buffers, disclaimers, or blaming.
2. Don't back down from the action you feel is appropriate, regardless of the reaction you get from your employee.

The Details

Don't apologize. This is not your fault. Your employee made commitments. She didn't follow through on them. You are not doing this "to" her. She, by her actions, has earned this action. Don't let her make you feel otherwise. While it's unfortunate that you both are in this situation, your employee is the one who put you both there. So don't say things like:

- "I'm sorry I have to do this, but I have to write you up."
- "Gosh, I really hate to have to do this, especially right before a long weekend, but . . ."
- "I'm sorry this has to happen, especially today of all days, but I have to . . ."

Remember, you are not punishing your employee. You are taking action that is designed to help him recommit and refocus on his goals for the organization. Also, remember that your action is intended to help him be successful, not hurt or punish him. If you are being fair, there is no need to apologize for the action you take.

Own the action you are taking. Don't blame your boss, human resources, company policy, the union agreement, or anything else for causing you to take action. Take responsibility for acting on behalf of your organization. Even if you are compelled to take this action by your boss or some company policy, own your action. You are an agent or a representative of your organization. Look at the following example:

You shouldn't say, "Our policy requires that I give you this write-up for lighting a cigarette outside the designated area. I think this is a little harsh, but my hands are tied."

Instead, own the action you take. You are an agent of your organization and sometimes may have to take action contrary to your personal opinion. It goes with the job. "You lit a cigarette in the hallway. That is outside the designated area. That violates our smoking rules and I am giving you this write-up."

Blaming others may give you a temporary feeling of camaraderie with your employee. But even if it does, that camaraderie is not worth the respect you lose from that person. Blaming also makes the action you take seem much less serious to your employee. This defeats much of the purpose.

Don't back down. You have managed this situation well. Your employee knew what was expected. She committed to it. She fell short. You owe it to your organization as well as to this employee to stand firm. Do not feel obliged to give her another chance, be a nice guy, have a little heart, give her a break, or otherwise turn back from the appropriate action. If you do, you stand to lose the respect of your employee. If others find out (which they may through this employee), you will lose their respect as well.

Respond to your employee's reaction. Listen and reply with empathy. Don't dwell here, though. Move quickly to the next step to focus on resolving the problem.

Step 5. Agree on a specific action plan.

The Reasons

A huge part of holding your employee accountable is to help him get back on track. After giving feedback and taking corrective action, you should now turn your focus to the future and what's most important: improving performance. An action plan will help you clarify expectations for the near future. View it as a "mini" Performance Plan.

The Basics

1. Coach your employee to develop an action plan rather than dictating one to him.
2. Brainstorm possible resolutions together.
3. Keep the responsibility with your employee, not yourself.

The Details

Follow these guidelines to formulate a good action plan.

Now is the time to be a good coach. Help your employee get back on track. Blaming, nitpicking, and finding fault are all counterproductive. They will not help your employee get ready to improve his performance.

Remind your employee that she still needs to reach the goals you originally laid out. Point out what's in it for her to meet those goals personally. Help her see that reaching her goals is in her own best interest.

Discuss together what it will look and feel like when your employee is successful. Energize your employee with the vision of a successful future.

Brainstorm possible solutions together. Consider any and all ideas that come up. Do not critique your employee's ideas initially; just accept them as possibilities. Try not to offer your own ideas until your employee has offered a few. Try to get him to think of more than one or two possible solutions. For instance:

- "What are some ideas you have that would get you back up to standard?"
- "How can you get a better handle on this situation?"
- "What are some of the things you can do to turn this problem around?"
- "What else?"

Evaluate all the ideas in relation to the goals your employee is trying to accomplish. Determine which are most likely to be successful. Don't settle on a solution just to have a solution. Struggle, if you must, until you find a solution that you both are confident will work.

Keep the responsibility on your employee. The problem belongs to the employee. The obligation to resolve it is also that person's. You are not duty-bound to find a solution. In your effort to help, do not overhelp. Don't solve the problem for the employee. Let her find a solution that will work. She will own the solution more if it comes from herself. When she owns it, she will be more committed to making it work and more likely to be successful. That's a win for you, your employee, and the organization.

If neither of you has any good ideas, it may help to take a break. Assign your employee to come up with a certain number of viable options before you meet next.

For your part, explore ways that you can remove roadblocks. Your employee probably cannot succeed on his own. Look for ways that you can help. While the responsibility to resolve the problem is your employee's, that doesn't mean that you have no responsibility. You are there to remove obstacles and offer support, as in:

- "I promise to sign authorization requests within 24 hours of receiving them from now on."
- "Would it help if we move the display unit over here?"
- "I can talk to the people in that division and ask them to supply you with the data earlier in the day."

Solutions should be in the SMART format. That way you can hold your employee accountable for results. In a sense, you have come full circle. This discussion is a mini-goal-setting discussion. Your employee must commit, once again, to meeting expectations that you will hold her accountable for achieving. Anything your employee commits to doing in this conversation must be specific, measurable, action-focused, realistic, and time-bound. "I'll try harder"

isn't enough. Accountability requires that you use the same principles here as before.

Set interim goals if your employee needs them. Interim goals may
be necessary when your employee is unable to meet his original
goals or expectations. Interim goals will help the person get closer
and closer to the original goals without having to get there in one
big step. Use interim goals sparingly. Aim to get your employee up
to the original goal or expectation quickly. Consider this example:

> Your employee is having trouble processing 14 claims per hour.
> He averages 10 per hour. An interim goal would be to get 11.5
> claims processed per hour for the next two weeks. After two
> weeks, you set another interim goal of 13 claims per hour. Even-
> tually, your employee is up to the minimum of 14 claims per
> hour.

If a project is off track, you may have to renegotiate one or more
of the goals with your employee. Again, interim goals may help.
Seek to get your employee back on track quickly. Remember, you
are not doing this "to" her; she has created this difficulty and you
are helping her find a way out. Be firm but realistic, even with
interim goals.

Step 6. Set a follow-up date and stick to it.

The Reasons
Use the follow-up to check and make sure your employee is keeping
the commitments he just made. Holding him accountable does not
happen in one discussion. It's ongoing.

A follow-up date will also reinforce for your employee how serious this is. It's serious enough that you will allot more of your time
to meet again, just to be sure things are getting back on track.

The Basics
1. Set a date to follow up with your employee on her action
   plan and any interim goals.

2. Stick to that date even if your employee's performance is stellar.

The Details

Here's how to set your follow-up date and get the most out of it.

Establish a follow-up date and be sure to keep it. The follow-up date is to review progress. This shows you are serious about what needs to happen. For instance:

> "Let's meet again next Tuesday at three o'clock. We can talk about your progress then. You should be on top of your backlog by then, right? So we'll confirm that, and then we'll be able to see if you're on track to meet your monthly production goal as well."

The discussion will be similar to ones in the past. Review what the goals are and compare actual performance to those goals following the guidelines in this book. Recognize the improvement if there is some. Discuss ongoing problems and decide either to stick with the plan you have or to adjust it to better suit both your needs.

Set the follow-up date based on the issue. Determine how long it will take before you can reasonably expect to see a change in behavior. Set the follow-up date for then. Err on the side of meeting too soon rather than too late. For example:

- A follow-up date one week later for the employee who is late coming back from break every other day may be too late.
- A follow-up date one week later for the employee who just had a fistfight with a co-worker may be too soon.

It is absolutely critical that you keep this follow-up date. Your employee may turn his or her performance around quickly. Busy as you are, you will be tempted to give a hasty "Keep it up!" and dismiss the follow-up meeting. Don't do it! Skipping the meeting will send the wrong message to your employee. You made a commitment to follow up. You said this was serious. Let your actions support your words.

Sit down and review his progress even if it's been outstanding. If he is hitting the goals, now is the time to recognize and reinforce the great performance. Be as specific and detailed with your positive feedback as you were with your constructive feedback.

When you do sit down and talk in more detail about any progress, you may find things aren't going quite as wonderfully as you thought. You may also uncover other issues looming on the horizon that are better to head off now than later. Keep the follow-up date.

Set more follow-up dates if necessary. Don't be afraid to overdo it with follow-ups. Better to overdo it and ensure success than to underdo it and have your employee's improvements not be sustained:

> "I'd like to meet with you every Wednesday, 15 minutes before the end of your shift. We can review your progress and make adjustments to your workload. We'll do this through the end of next month. I want us both to be confident that you can handle the new process on your own before I step away completely, okay?"

Step 7. Offer your support.

The Reasons

You care about this employee. You want her to be successful. As her manager, you have a responsibility to support her as she works to improve her performance. It may be obvious to you, but not so obvious to your employee. She needs to hear it and feel it.

The Basics

1. Offer your help and support.
2. Do not take on your employee's responsibility to resolve the problem.
3. Tell your employee that you're confident he can reach his goals.

The Details

Here's how best to give support so that it benefits everyone.

Make your offer of help and support explicit. No matter how positively you've been holding her accountable, it is likely that your employee's experience has not been totally positive. She needs to hear you express your desire to help and support her. Using her name helps your offer come across as even more personal and sincere. Try saying things like:

- "I'm here to help you, Wayne."
- "I'm right here behind you, Nikki. I will support you all the way."
- "Alex, please don't hesitate to let me know if you need help."

Make yourself available to clarify issues, answer questions, or otherwise help your employee. You may even want to give him an overview of your availability for the next week or so.

Support your employee, but do not take over his responsibility. Too much help from you is a disservice to your employee. Step back and let him shoulder the work. His sense of pride will be genuine when he succeeds on his own.

Express your confidence that your employee can turn this situation around. End on a positive note now with a word of encouragement. Don't gush; just say what you sincerely think and feel, then leave it at that. Here are some examples:

- "We've worked together long enough for me to know that you have it in you to be a great salesperson. I know you can meet next month's quota. I'm behind you 100 percent!"
- "I'm confident that if you put your mind to it, you'll be able to meet your quota next month."

Say what feels genuine and sincere. You do not have to be a cheerleader; just express your confidence.

Step 8. Document the discussion.

The Reasons

You'll want to refer back to this discussion as you coach your employee to improve her performance. You both are not likely to remember the discussion the same way, so make a record of the salient points.

The Basics

1. Check with your boss or human resources rep before finalizing your notes into documentation of the discussion. Your organization may have specific formats, guidelines, or other policies that apply.
2. Record what you discussed *after*, not before, the discussion.
3. Share the document with your employee.

The Details

Here are some specific ways to document the discussion with your employee.

Documentation should include:

- The date of your discussion
- The names of everyone present (you, your employee, a shop steward, etc.)
- A brief summary of the feedback that you gave your employee
- The plan of action that your employee committed to follow
- What you committed to do to support your employee
- A follow-up date
- Future action possible if the issue is not resolved
- A brief statement expressing your confidence in your employee's ability to resolve the issue

You will use this document like a Performance Plan—to hold your employee accountable for the results he committed to achieving. He can refer to it to keep himself focused.

Share this document with your employee. You want her to confirm that it accurately reflects what was said. If you skip this step, you risk an argument about the documentation somewhere down the road when both your memories are fuzzier. You may need to adjust the wording or other minor elements to accommodate how your employee saw the discussion. This is fine as long as you do not lose the essence of what happened with the edited document. Present the document and say something like:

> "Would you look at this? It's a record of what we talked about earlier today. I hope you agree that it reflects what we discussed. But if it is missing anything or doesn't truly reflect what happened as you remember it, please tell me so that we can make any necessary changes."

Don't be discouraged with a disagreement over the document. Disagreement just validates the need for a document in the first place. If the two of you remember the same discussion so differently now, imagine how much more different your perspectives would be a week, a month, or a year from now. Better to have the clarifying conversations now than later.

If you find yourselves completely at odds over the documentation, perhaps you need to have the discussion all over again. Clarify periodically throughout the second conversation. Take notes as you discuss things and write down each agreement you make as you make it.

Document the discussion after you have it, not before. Walking into the discussion with a document already written up suggests that you are not open to input or other information that may truly change the action you are taking. Even if you state up front that this is "only a draft," the message will be that your mind is already made up.

Bringing a document with you changes the focus of the discussion. The focus will shift to the document itself: the contents, the wording, and even your intended distribution of it. You are more likely to end up reading the letter than talking. Your employee is more apt to close up. None of these encourages a productive problem-solving discussion.

This doesn't mean you should not come to the discussion with notes. You may want those notes to help you remember the points that you want to make or the facts of the situation. Do not hesitate to write some notes while you have the conversation either. Bringing notes and taking notes will help you stay focused. Both will also help you document your discussion more precisely. Both send the message to your employee that this is serious.

Check with your boss or human resources department before you share documentation with your employee. Your organization may have a preferred format or a hierarchy of approvals that goes along with such documentation. Distribute copies per your organization's prescribed guidelines.

EXAMPLE: Link to Consequences Discussion

Manager: We need to talk about your punctuality, Ben. Since we last talked, you have been late two more times. On July 17, you were 35 minutes late. Then today you were 20 minutes late. What's going on?

Employee: I know. I know. I should be on time. Trust me, it won't happen again!

Manager: I'm glad to hear you want to correct the problem, but we have talked about this before. So I'd like to take a closer look at this. What's actually causing you to be late?

Employee: Well, the traffic has really been bad lately . . .

Manager: I see. So it's the traffic causing you to be so late?

Employee: Yeah. Well, kind of . . . Actually, it's really more like my car and the traffic. It keeps stalling in traffic. You know, like at a stop light or something. My brother-in-law was supposed to fix it last week, but he got some free tickets to the races, so he did that instead. Anyway, he should be able to look at it next weekend. Just give me a little more time, okay? He's really great with cars and I'm sure he'll get it all fixed up by then.

Manager: Hmm, car trouble is no fun! And I'm guessing you don't like being the one holding up traffic any more than you like being late to work. Is that right? Still, you did make a commitment to me last week that you would be at work on time every day. What can you do to make sure that happens from now on?

Employee: Wow, I don't know. It's not really that big of a deal, though, you know. I've only been late once or twice a week, and I'm not very late—just a few minutes or so. Besides, the rest of the group is more than happy to pitch in until I get here. We have a great team, you know.

Manager: Well, you're right. We do have a great team here. And they do rally to get the job done when necessary. I just don't think it's fair to depend on them to cover for you when you are late for work, especially when it's as many times as we have had to lately, do you? Despite their efforts, your team members aren't able to accommodate all the calls that would have gone to you, either. So we see a higher "call-abandonment rate" when you're here. Ben, you're an important member of this team. We all feel the loss when you're not here contributing with us. Do you see that?

Employee: Yeah, I guess so . . .

Manager: Good. Then what can you do to make sure that you are on time from now on?

Employee: Well, like I said, my brother-in-law is going to take a look at the car next week. I'm sure he'll get it fixed then, so you won't have to worry anymore.

Manager: I hope he can fix it for you, Ben. But what about until that happens?

Employee: I don't know. I guess I'll just have to pray that the darn thing doesn't stall between now and then!

Manager: I was hoping that we could come up with a plan that relied on something a little bit more in your control.

Employee: Well, what should I do, then?

Manager: I don't know, Ben. This is not my problem. I think you are in a better position to think up ways to get yourself to work on time than I am. You know your situation better. Surely you can come up with a solution for the interim until your car is fixed. What do you think?

Employee: *(After a long pause)* Well, I guess there's always public transportation. Although I doubt any buses stop near my place.

Manager: Good idea. A few buses stop right in front of the building here, so that may be just the answer. Okay now, what if that doesn't work?

Employee: Hmm, well, I don't know. I'll just have to hope it does . . . Okay, well, if worse comes to worst I guess I could catch a ride with someone else. Either that or maybe I can work something out with my sister.

Manager: Good. It sounds like you have several options to explore, Ben. I'm sure you'll be able to select the one that will work best for you. Just to summarize, then: You will follow up next week with your brother-in-law about getting him to fix your car. In the meantime, you will either use the bus to get to work on time, or you will work out getting a ride with someone else, maybe your sister. Ben, because we've already talked about this issue a couple of times, this discussion will constitute a formal oral warning. An oral warning is the first step in our Corrective Action Process. I will write a brief summary of our conversation. I will give you a copy, and I will put another copy in your file. Assuming that you are able to get to work on time from now on, we won't need to discuss this again. After six months, I will remove the letter from your file and destroy it. If the problem persists, however, I will have to take further corrective action—a written warning. Ben, I am confident that you will be able to manage your transportation to work from now on. If the options that you're looking at don't pan out for you, let's get back together again and see if we can come up with some more alternatives, okay? In fact, why don't we just plan on getting together in a few days to discuss your plans and check on your progress? How about at 3:00 P.M. on Monday?

Employee: Okay, sure. I guess that's a good idea.

Manager: Great. I'll be anxious to hear how you're able to solve this problem, Ben.

EXAMPLE: Link to Consequences Documentation

July 21

Dear Ben:

This memo documents our meeting of July 20, when we discussed ongoing concerns about your being late to work. Since our last discussion on July 12, you have been more than 15 minutes late to work twice, on July 17 and July 20. We agreed that your being late for work puts an unfair burden on your coworkers and that it often increases our call-abandonment rate when you are not available.

At the meeting, you said that your lateness for work was primarily due to car problems that would be fixed within two weeks. In the meantime, you said that you would look into public transportation options immediately and use one if it's feasible. If not, you committed to make other ride arrangements to make sure that you get to work on time from now on.

I told you that our discussion constituted an oral warning in our Corrective Action Process, and that a copy of this memo would be kept in your file for at least six months. If you continue to come to work late, you will subject yourself to the next corrective step of a written warning.

Ben, I am confident you can resolve the transportation issues that affect your punctuality. We will meet again at 3:00 P.M. on July 23 to review your progress in this area.

Sincerely,

Manager

Checklist: Link to Consequences

❏ I select consequences that I believe will best help my employees improve their performance.

❏ I avoid actions that do nothing more than punish.

❏ I remind my employees of commitments made and check to be sure they also remember these commitments.

❏ I clearly and directly explain what action I am taking.

❏ I clearly and directly explain why I am taking that action.

❏ I do not apologize for, blame others for, or otherwise disown the action I take.

❏ I encourage my employees to create an action plan to resolve problems. I give input without taking over.

❏ I set a follow-up date so I can continue to hold my employees accountable for progress toward their goals.

❏ I sincerely offer support and express my confidence in my employees' ability to get their jobs done.

❏ I document the discussion after we've had it, so our focus stays on the problem and not on the document.

❏ I record our discussion to reflect our agreements and commitments, and I share this document with my employees.

CHAPTER 6

✓Evaluate Effectiveness

No process is complete without an evaluation. After you have worked with the principles of accountability for a while, evaluate how your efforts have paid off. Determine how successful you are at holding your employees accountable to reach the goals that you've set. Also review how you handled the process. Find ways to become more effective at applying the principles of accountability.

Step 1. Hold yourself accountable for *what* you accomplished.

The Reasons

Your main job as a manager is to get work done through others. What your employees accomplish is probably one of your own goals, which your own manager will hold you accountable for. Your own manager will be duly impressed if you do this work for her by holding yourself accountable for your employees' success.

Holding yourself accountable sets an example for your employees to follow. You will have a tough time holding others accountable if you do not hold yourself accountable.

The Basics

1. Review what your employees' goals are.
2. Review what your employees' results are.

3. Where they have been successful, determine why.
4. Where they have been unsuccessful, determine why.
5. Apply your findings to "next time."

The Details

Go back through this book for yourself. Change "your employees" to "you," apply the principles, and hold yourself accountable. If it'll work for them, it'll work for you!

Step 2. Hold yourself accountable for *how* you accomplished it.

The Reasons

Your main job as a manager is to get work done through others. Your primary tools for doing this are the principles of accountability. You become a more effective manager when you evaluate how you applied each principle and determine where you did well and where you stand to improve.

The Basics

1. Evaluate how well you've set expectations with SMART goals.
2. Evaluate how well you've invited commitment, not just acceptance.
3. Evaluate how well you've measured results fairly and accurately.
4. Evaluate how well you've provided feedback that didn't provoke a defensive reaction.
5. Evaluate how well you've linked results to consequences that helped your employees.
6. Evaluate how well you've documented each step in the process.

The Details

How will you hold yourself accountable?

◆ *Ask your boss or a trusted colleague to help you hold yourself accountable for these principles.* That person can use the checklists at the end of each chapter (also listed below) to confirm your success. She or he will help you stay unbiased in your self-assessment by questioning and challenging your responses.

Getting help has another benefit. This person will see your example and learn from it. Indirectly, you will help spread the concept of quality accountability in your organization.

◆ *Your documentation may protect your organization.* Somewhere down the line, if it is determined that an employee is not a good match for his job, your documentation will be valuable. It will show that a good-faith effort was made to help that employee meet the standards and expectations of that job.

Accountability Checklists

Evaluate: Set Expectations

❏ I understand what my organization wants to accomplish by having reviewed its mission, vision, values, and strategies.

❏ I know what part of my organization's success is my team's responsibility, and I wholeheartedly accept that responsibility.

❏ I know what I will hold each of my employees responsible for. All of their individual responsibilities add up to the whole of what our team is collectively responsible for.

❏ My employees are either writing their own goals, or they are significantly helping me write them in the SMART format.

❏ Each goal is Specific. They are all clear, unambiguous, and focused. I've avoided labels and generalizations.

❏ Each goal is Measurable. I can count what I expect for each goal. I've avoided measures that are subjective and vague.

❏ Each goal is Action-oriented. They focus on behaviors, actions, and results. I've avoided trying to measure attitudes and intentions.

❏ Each goal is Realistic. My employees and I believe they can each be achieved. I've avoided asking for perfection and the unattainable.

❏ It is Realistic to expect all the goals together to be achieved in the time frame given.

❏ Each goal is Time-bound. I know when each must be completed. I've avoided making assumptions about priorities and urgencies.

Evaluate: Invite Commitment

❏ I can explain why my employees' goals exist. I can make the direct link between each goal and our organization's direction.

❏ I can show each employee what is in it for him personally to achieve his goals.

❏ I understand what motivates each employee from within, and I am able to help her get that buzz from her own success.

❏ I have developed or plan to use incentives that I know will appeal to my employees' needs and wants (which may differ from my own).

❏ I have resolved any concerns I had about their goals.

❏ I am ready and eager to discuss goals with my employees in an environment that is conducive to such a discussion.

❏ I am ready for my employees' reactions to their goals, even if the reactions are negative. I am confident that I can get them to fully understand their goals.

❏ I am ready to ask my employees for buy-in or commitment to their goals. I will recognize their positive response when I hear it.

❏ I know how to turn an "acceptance" response to goals into a commitment.

❏ I am confident about handling any "rejection" response I may hear.

❏ I will have my employee document our discussion and agreement about goals in a Performance Plan.

❏ Each employee and I will keep a copy of the Performance Plan.

❏ We will revisit the Performance Plan periodically to keep it up-to-date and relevant.

Evaluate: Measure Results

❏ Our measurement tools are efficient. We are not spending more on them than is necessary.

❏ Our measurement tools are fair. The data accurately measures what it is supposed to measure.

❏ Our measurement tools are simple. In most, if not all cases, they are automated to allow employees to stay focused on their jobs.

❏ I record the data collected and I share the data as it becomes available.

❏ I appropriately share data to promote healthy competition among my workers.

❏ I compare the data collected from my employees' performance with the goals to identify gaps.

❏ I identify and understand the impact the data suggests.

Evaluate: Provide Feedback

❏ I understand not only how my employees will gain from receiving my feedback, but also how I will benefit by giving it.

❏ I give feedback as soon as possible after I observe the behavior or action, making sure my employees are ready to hear it.

❏ I always give constructive feedback in private. I may give positive feedback in public when I'm confident that my employees would appreciate that.

❏ I set the stage for a positive interaction before jumping into giving feedback.

❑ I describe specifically what I observed, sticking to what actually transpired without adding judgment, comment, or analysis.

❑ I avoid making generalizations and using words like *always* and *never*.

❑ I avoid talking about attitudes, intentions, or labels in place of behaviors and actions.

❑ I avoid using the word *but*.

❑ I explain objectively the impact my employees' behavior had on the organization.

❑ I seek to understand my employees' perspective of the situation.

❑ I offer a suggestion for how to improve only if my employees truly need one or ask for one.

Evaluate: Link to Consequences

❑ I select consequences that I believe will best help my employees improve their performance.

❑ I avoid actions that do nothing more than punish.

❑ I remind my employees of commitments made and check to be sure they also remember these commitments.

❑ I clearly and directly explain what action I am taking.

❑ I clearly and directly explain why I am taking that action.

❑ I do not apologize for, blame others for, or otherwise disown the action I take.

❑ I encourage my employees to create an action plan to resolve problems. I give input without taking over.

❑ I set a follow-up date so I can continue to hold my employees accountable for progress toward their goals.

❑ I sincerely offer support and express my confidence in my employees' ability to get their jobs done.

❑ I document the discussion after we've had it, so our focus stays on the problem and not on the document.

❑ I record our discussion to reflect our agreements and commitments, and I share this document with my employees.

ABOUT THE AUTHOR

Brian Cole Miller, founder of Working Solutions (www.busymanager .com), is the author of *Quick Team-Building Activities for Busy Managers*. A sought-after speaker and trainer, Brian specializes in building more competent and confident leaders, especially at the front line. He has provided training, coaching, and consulting to busy managers internationally, including those at Nationwide Insurance, Communications Workers of America, Anthem Blue Cross Blue Shield, and UPS.